GLIMPSING RESURRECTION

DEANNA A. THOMPSON

GLIMPSING RESURRECTION

Cancer, Trauma, and Ministry

WESTMINSTER
JOHN KNOX PRESS
LOUISVILLE · KENTUCKY

First edition
Published by Westminster John Knox Press
Louisville, Kentucky

18 19 20 21 22 23 24 25 26 27—10 9 8 7 6 5 4 3 2 1

Book design by Drew Stevens
Cover design by Nita Ybarra

Library of Congress Cataloging-in-Publication Data

Names: Thompson, Deanna A., 1966– author.
Title: Glimpsing resurrection : cancer, trauma, and ministry / Deanna A. Thompson.
Description: First edition. | Louisville, Kentucky : Westminster John Knox Press, 2018. |
    Includes bibliographical references and index. | Identifiers: LCCN 2018006341 (print) |
    LCCN 2018022755 (ebook) | ISBN 9781611648829 (ebk.) | ISBN 9780664262761
    (pbk. : alk. paper)
Subjects: LCSH: Cancer—Religious aspects—Christianity. | Cancer—Patients—Religious
    life. | Death—Religious aspects—Christianity. | Resurrection. | Thompson, Deanna A.,
    1966– | Cancer—Patients—United States—Biography.
Classification: LCC BV4910.33 (ebook) | LCC BV4910.33 .T4595 2018 (print) |
    DDC 248.8/6196994—dc23
LC record available at https://lccn.loc.gov/2018006341

To all those undone by cancer
who dare to hope for more

CONTENTS

Foreword by Willie James Jennings   ix

Acknowledgments   xv

Introduction   1

1. Undone by Cancer   11

2. Living with Trauma Brought on by Illness   43

3. Trauma, Illness, and the Christian Story   71

4. Church for the Undone   119

5. Not-Yet-Resurrection Hope   147

   Notes   163

   Index   181

FOREWORD

Undone and Redone

The makeup of our psyche or our systems of support really do not matter; we can be undone. Pain and suffering deconstructs us. It pulls us apart. This is the reality of being creatures created out of nothing. We have no inherent stability, no bodily mechanism that guarantees eternality. The truth of the creation and of every living creature is our contingency. We did not have to be; but because we are, we are loved by God, our creator. The real question that flows out of such knowledge is "How can we live with such knowledge?" This is a different question than questions of theodicy.

Theodicy questions revolve around the idea that God—as the all-powerful and controlling progenitor of all that exists—is in some fundamental way responsible for pain and suffering. This concept begets another tragic idea: that God observes our pain and suffering and could do something about it, if God wished to do so; but for reasons beyond our understanding, God does not act on our behalf. Theodicy questions circle these ideas, drawing energy from them. Such questions always drive people into endless, exhausting searches for answers that they will never find, because theodicy questions are always self-enclosed. Theodicy questions are bad questions. I write this not in any way intending to be insensitive or theologically elitist but fully recognizing the folly of questions that flow out of ideas of an abstract, all-powerful, and controlling God bound to realities of inexplicable and explicable human suffering and pain.

The problem is not that we ask questions of God in the face of pain and suffering. The problem is that we are often trapped in asking the wrong kinds of questions, questions that are in league with our becoming undone and allied with our deconstruction. The task of Christian theology and the calling of Christian community is to help people ask the right kinds of questions. This is our birthright and our great joy found deeply inside the character of Christian witness. We theologians, for our part, dance constantly with the questioning—stepping now this way and now another, avoiding death-dealing questions, moving quickly toward life-producing questions—always seeking to discern the difference in questions, always watching for questions that start off badly but then move toward the good or questions that begin with the best of intentions but quickly become toxic. This is not heroic work because theologians are surely not heroes. We are only those who are called to give witness with all the people of God to a God who has joined the divine life to the life of the creature. We testify that the God who creates has been joined to the creature that questions.

A creating God and a questioning creature are meant for each other. This is the logic of love born of the creation itself. God planned for communion and aimed for a reciprocal speaking and hearing: "Come now, let us argue it out, says the LORD" (Isa. 1:18a). The divine desire for communion is not the reason for our pain and suffering. It is God's response to that pain and suffering. In becoming human, in bearing and being the story of Israel in Jesus of Nazareth, God has turned our questions toward communion. This is the heart of the matter. The difference between good and bad questions pivot around communion. Those questions that drive us away from sensing the heart of God for us are bad questions, not by their quality, character, or texture, or even their intensity, but by their direction. They are not aimed at the real God but at a fiction, a fantasy of

God — all-powerful and inscrutable, who weaves together mystery with maliciousness. Good questions are intense and personal, urgent and angry, and relentless, always wanting to hear and know, see and sense God responding. Such questions begin with the real God: a God who is touched with the infirmities of the creature and the creation, acquainted with grief, familiar with sorrow and with very bad news. This real God found in Jesus knows rejection, isolation, relentless pain, and what it feels like to be undone. Starting from this sure knowledge of this real God, the triune God given to us in Jesus Christ, the real questions can begin, and a struggle that is itself already redemptive comes into view.

To make a struggle redemptive is not to glorify it, and certainly not to imagine it as a providential plan of God, but to allow it to be a struggle with God, bound up in God's own life with us. I constantly tell my students, those aiming to be a pastoral presence to suffering people, that coming alongside people as they ask questions of God and as they struggle with suffering and pain is one of the greatest privileges of Christian ministry. It is an art of ministry to know how to help people form and articulate their own questions in ways that draw them toward communion with God. It is an art that demands a lifetime of cultivation through patiently listening to people and yielding to the Holy Spirit who guides us into truth. This brings me to the work of theological writing, writing at the sites of hurting people who are sincerely and honestly asking questions.

Writing theology is always difficult work, because it is such an audacious act. Who would dare write about God and write in the aftermath of the word of God — spoken, written, preached, and embodied? Who would dare imagine that they could write about all creatures and the creaturely condition as a singular creature? And who would dare write about the intercourse of divine word and beloved creatures with confidence, assured that they had a duty and a calling to do so. Only theologians write like this. When we do, we find we must live with the consequences, such as (a) being ignored and sometimes ridiculed by other intellectuals who think such writing is ridiculous; and

(b) standing under the judgment of a God who considers every word we say, especially to and about those who suffer. Yet there is another dynamic that marks the writing of a theologian: we write as fragile bodies even as we write about fragile bodies. Some theologians forget this dynamic, and their writing shows that forgetfulness. These are those whose lust for cleverness and a sterile articulation overwhelms the creaturely nature of theological witness. They become a talking head. There are, however, other theologians who never forget that they are fully body. Admittedly, it takes a special theologian, a stunning Christian intellectual, to write at the site of pain and suffering while being themselves a site of pain and suffering.

This kind of writing cannot be adequately captured with the label of "autobiography," because something richer and far denser than memoir happens with such writing. It has the character of the one speaking with the many, and the feeling of a multitude and a single life merged together without the one ever canceling out the other. The best theological writing about suffering has this character, but unfortunately such writing is rare. Fortunately for us, Deanna Thompson writes in this way and has been doing so for a long time. Theologian Thompson brings a beautiful precision to an engagement with pain and suffering through her focus on cancer. She has needed such focus in order to struggle with cancer's undoing of her life.

Deanna Thompson gives us words to fight against cancer. Her words fight against the way the diagnosis of and struggle against cancer can destroy our souls and strangle us in despair. Thompson, the extraordinary theologian and cancer survivor, allows her words to give powerful witness to God's words and, in so doing, has written a book for the ages. As long as people fight against cancer and as long as theologians, pastors, and congregants have to think through cancer with their faith, Deanna Thompson's book will be a celebrated ally and a welcome friend. But Thompson's words will also help people find their way to the right questions to ask God and the best ways to position their struggles as a shared project with God, even and especially if they imagine they struggle against God.

There is no sin in imagining that we struggle against God in our suffering. God will not be our enemy in such imaginings but will through the Holy Spirit seek to reveal the divine life joined to our suffering. The Apostles' Creed teaches us to confess that "Jesus descended." We serve a God made known to us in Jesus Christ who has claimed the spot at the bottom: at the deepest places of anger and shame, of exhaustion and frustration, of despair and abandonment, where there is no possibility of digging a deeper hole or of grasping even more nothingness. Jesus descended to that place, and he will meet us there with the power of a God who will not let the descending be the last action. Being there with Jesus is the beginnings of our resurrection. This will be the first action of a new life—life eternal. The body will be redone. And even in the depths of despair with him, we can glimpse what is to come.

Willie James Jennings

ACKNOWLEDGMENTS

This book would not have come into being without the wisdom, guidance, and help of so many. To the following I'm especially grateful:

Shelly Rambo, for grabbing coffee in Nashville's Scarritt Bennett dining hall and inviting me to talk and write about illness-related trauma for your project on post-traumatic public theology; for the conferences in Boston, Amsterdam, and St. Paul, where the discussions continued; and for your support and guidance for the Louisville Institute grant. Your generous approach to expanding the conversation on trauma and theology changed the course of my research and is making a difference in people's lives.

Willie James Jennings, for saying to that room full of theologians at the Boston School of Theology that the work I was doing on illness-related trauma was important; for your recommendation to the Louisville Institute on my behalf; and for ongoing conversations over e-mail, in airport terminals, and beyond. Your friendship and support have energized this project all the way along.

The Louisville Institute, for a Sabbatical Grant for Researchers that helped fund my 2016–2017 sabbatical and to all the fabulous members of group A at the institute's winter seminar in January 2017, most especially Jessica Coblentz for your sea-parting feedback on where my project was headed and for your willingness to read more of the project and join me and the consultants in workshopping the draft in the Hamline faculty lounge in the spring of 2017. The project is richer because of your insights.

Todd Billings, JoAnn Post, Monica Coleman, and Shelly Rambo, for signing on as consultants to the project through the Louisville Institute grant. Our conversation on that early spring morning in the faculty lounge over coffee, muffins, and fruit helped me build the confidence that I was on the right track and prompted me to shift course in several significant ways. To be with you all in that space of considering the intersections of trauma, illness, and theology was one of the most powerful experiences of my professional life. Thank you for your presence and your wisdom on those March days, not just for our morning workshopping but for each of your engagements in our symposium on religious responses to trauma, illness, and healing.

Deborah and George Hunsinger, for the serendipitous conversations about trauma and theology at the Academy of Parish Clergy conference in Florida that winter several years ago—your generous thinking with me about this fledgling project continues to inform my thinking.

The Collegeville Institute and Lauren Winner, for facilitating that transformational writing workshop in summer 2016 that offered the gifts of space, time, and direction needed to jumpstart this project. And to our fantastic cohort of writers, whose generous daily engagement around that seminar table about our writing and our lives nourished me in the months to come. A special shout-out to Kate Bowler for continuing our Collegeville conversations virtually, and for our sacred walk and talk about trauma and cancer along San Antonio's Riverwalk and a most memorable breakfast at Mickey's Diner that cold St. Paul morning. If we have to be traveling this incurable cancer path, I'm so grateful for your companionship.

Hamline University, for granting me a year-long sabbatical, and to chaplain Nancy Victorin-Vangerud, the Wesley Center, and Mahle Endowment, for a year of co-planning and carrying out the "Healing, Wholeness, and Holiness" symposium at Hamline in March 2017. And for all symposium participants, especially Rolf Jacobson, John Hermanson, Eric Weiss, and Sherry Jordan for their inspiring collaboration and participation, and for teaching me and others about life and faith and hope amid life-threatening illness.

Andy Tix, for your generous sharing of knowledge of and expertise in psychological research on trauma, for reading and commenting on drafts of this project, and for several wonderfully helpful conversations over tea in St. Paul about how psychology and theology might talk to each other in this project and beyond.

Pastor Bradley Schmeling, for your friendship and your insights on what it's like to walk with those who live with life-threatening illness and to cultivate practices of worship that make space for being undone and for expressions of healing; and to Gloria Dei Lutheran Church in St. Paul, my home congregation, for the opportunity to try out the ideas in this book and for the encouragement and support from so many for the work I do.

Mount Olivet Lutheran Church in Minneapolis, whose invitations to speak on topics related to this project helped shape and form what appears on these pages.

Deborah Jones from Allina Health's LifeCourse, for our many months of living-room conversations about what it's like to live long(er) and even well with advanced-stage cancer and for all the insight and resources you and Rev. Katie provided for me for this project.

Diane Erickson, for the conversations about trauma and cancer and for all the links and articles you sent me throughout spring and summer 2017; this project has been enriched by your insights.

My parents, Rev. Mervin and Jackie Thompson, whose attendance at the Hamline symposium and other presentations on the topics in this book have offered helpful encouragement for the work I'm doing, not to mention the continued gifts of food after my ongoing treatments, along with daily dosages of prayer.

And most significantly, my daughters, Annika and Linnea Peterson, and my dear husband, Neal Peterson, whose consistent love and support have made it possible to endure the worst and hope for more to life, in this world and the next.

INTRODUCTION

In December of 2008, I was diagnosed with stage-IV breast cancer. Life became virtually unrecognizable; I went from being a healthy, active forty-two-year-old wife, mother, daughter, sister, professor, neighbor, and friend to being a virtual invalid with a life and family in crisis and a lousy prognosis for the future. By the time I was diagnosed with metastatic breast cancer, the cancer had spread from breast to bones, fracturing two vertebrae and camping out in my pelvis and hips. The intense treatment regimen radiologists put me on made me even sicker, leading to trips to the ER and a New Year's Eve in the hospital where my husband and I ushered in a new year by making plans for where I would be buried.

While family and friends immediately sought out statistics on my prognosis, it took being weaned off oxycodone before it occurred to me to hunt down those numerical predictors of my future: the statistics that said that five years out, 80 percent of people who have what I have are dead. I'm a religion professor, an expert talker who gets paid to talk about God. But being diagnosed with a *breast* cancer that crushes vertebrae and comes with sobering prospects about living long or well with the disease conspired against me. I had trouble locating words for this kind of cancer, trouble with words for (or *directed at*) God, trouble with words about the possibility of living with or in spite of it.

Effects of treatment and back surgery made death's nearness seem stiflingly close. I had trouble getting out of bed and dressing myself; I couldn't drive to and from the mountains of appointments. I resigned from virtually every part of my full and wonderful life, and I struggled to get back in the classroom to teach one final course. I hoped it would bring some closure to me and the campus community I loved so much. That classroom seemed to be the only space where cancer did not dictate all the terms of my life. Outside those three hours a week where I played the role of teacher, I was a cancer patient who seemed to have little time left.

When I cried my way through an entire oncology appointment, my oncologist suggested that I visit a cancer counselor to help me cope with my new life. The cancer counselor encouraged me to write letters to my preteen daughters that they could open on their graduations and wedding days where I expressed how much I wished I could be there to celebrate their special days.

But as winter turned to spring, the pain from back surgery receded enough for me to remove the Fentanyl patch on my arm and begin physical therapy. My twelve-year-old received an award at school for persevering in the face of adversity. I started driving again and found the energy to make a couple of meals a week. The back brace that had held my spine together moved to the attic, and at the beginning of summer, we resumed our tradition of family bike rides to a local lake. After months of being overwhelmed by the incurable status of my cancerous life and fearing the end was near, I went into remission—a lovely, disorienting state of being.

Friends and family threw me the party of a lifetime, and I interpreted my cancer story in light of the dominant version of the Christian story I had come to know so well:

And in this feasting amid the crying and the grieving, my life mapped the movement of the Christian gospel story in a way I never imaged it could: I have experienced first-hand a death and a resurrection. I have witnessed new life growing out of the ashes of death and destruction. It doesn't get more Christian than that.[1]

For months following my diagnosis, it looked like my stage-IV cancer story would swallow me whole. When it didn't, it was the Christian story that helped make sense of what had happened. Dawn had come. I had been given new life.

Yet in the past nine years, I have lost and found remission again and again. And while any day with remission is better than any day without it, there are many days when the death-to-new-life story line seems too constricted to hold the frayed edges of life with cancer. From the earliest days of my cancer story, the diagnosis-treatment-survivorship plotline also has seemed too streamlined, too linear to allow enough space for the incurable version I'm living. The fickle status of remission and the ongoing oncology visits and chemo treatments leave me searching for more spacious versions of the stories that interpret my life.

Before cancer, my work as a theologian and academic focused largely on questions of justice; I'm a Lutheran, feminist scholar who teaches religion through the lenses of gender and race. My family and I are part of a community of faith that understands the call of the gospel as a call to stand with those whose lives bear the marks of injustice. But getting sick has opened me to a world of hurt that can be hard to see and hear when our notions of the Christian story, Christian community, and Christian mission are cast primarily within a moral framework of justice. Don't get me wrong: I'm not interested in *less* focus on justice. But I am interested in cultivating greater consciousness of the suffering that *simply is* so that we can make more space for it, not just within our tellings of the Christian story but also in our embodiments of Christian community and our sense of what it means to share the burdens of those who suffer.

Illness, Anomie, and the Christian Story

Each of our lives bears the marks of suffering, and when we face intense experiences of suffering, we crave explanations for the *"Why?"*—answers for why things happen the way they do. Knowing why reassures us that we live in a *nomos*, an orderly world that operates according to understandable laws. We want life to make sense. We want things to happen for a reason. Society and religion provide us with what scholars call nomic structures within which we make sense of our world and the subplots of our lives.[2]

It is not surprising, then, that dominant versions of the cancer story strive toward nomos by placing life with serious illness in a moral framework. Those of us who live with cancer are cast in the role of warriors called on to battle the cancer with all the ammunition we've got. Telling cancer stories through the use of military images provides a logical framework for illnesses like cancer: cancer gets cast as an evil invader, and those of us who have the disease are called to take the moral high ground by fighting and ultimately defeating it.

It's also not surprising that a moral framework tends to remain in place when the cancer story meets up with the Christian story. The question of why becomes an insistent one. *Why* would a good God who overcomes moral evil allow illnesses like cancer to exist? Where's the justice in diagnoses of cancer? We crave nomic answers from a religion built around just conceptions of God, but when we pay attention to the lives of those with life-threatening illness—whether they are religious or not—the most insistent question tends less to be "Why?"—for so many of us, there's simply no logical explanation for why we were stricken with serious illness—than "How?"—as in "How do I live into this reality that is now my life?" For those of us who claim the Christian story as *our* story, the most pressing question becomes "How does the Christian story offer a framework of meaning to this cancer-filled life where meaning is constantly under threat?"

When events like a cancer diagnosis occur in the absence of any clear explanations, we are confronted with *anomos*, an unordered, unstructured, even lawless sense of the world. Unexplainable evil, or that which seems to be unexplainable, threatens the nomos by which we make sense of our lives. What's needed in our theologies is more space in the tellings of the Christian story—as well as in communal enactments of that story and the living out of the story's call to care for those who suffer—for the anomie that comes from living with serious illness.[3]

Pauline Boss, whose research on those who live with ambiguous loss—loss that lacks finality and resolution—suggests that the challenge in these situations is to bring clarity to an ambiguous situation. Failing that, and Boss notes that in most cases our attempts at clarity *will fail*, "the critical question is how to live with ambiguous loss."[4] The hope is that we can learn to live amid the loss, balancing our grief over the chaos that serious illness ushers into our lives with a recognition of what kind of living is still possible. It is my claim that using the lens of trauma to help understand losses brought to us by cancer will aid us in balancing the grief with a vision of how to go on, even amid enduring loss.

Trauma and Cancer

Trauma is "the suffering that remains"[5] in the aftermath of events in people's lives that threaten to overwhelm their ability to function. The growing field of trauma studies[6] is helping develop a deeper appreciation of how experiences of trauma foster that sense of anomie. Research documents how the invisible psychic wounds of trauma disorient and upend the lives of those who have endured awful events.

In the 1990s, life-threatening illness was added to the list of events and conditions that can cause post-traumatic stress disorder (PTSD).[7] In so doing, psychiatrists were acknowledging that the threat to life and bodily integrity due to cancer or other serious illnesses can precipitate deep senses of fear, devastation, and lack of control—all symptoms of post-traumatic stress. But applying a post-traumatic stress diagnosis to those who live with life-threatening illness remains an unsettled issue, as there are ways in which trauma associated with illness does not fit neatly into the diagnostic framework of post-traumatic stress. While conventional understandings of traumatic events focus on extraordinary occurrences in the past that have a beginning, middle, and end,[8] trauma associated with illness typically does not arise from a single event but rather from recurring events extending from diagnosis through treatment and beyond, possibly throughout the rest of a person's life.[9] Given this reality for people living with serious illness, researchers wonder whether those living with cancer can ever become "post-trauma."[10] The distinctive manifestations of cancer-related trauma reveal that the precise nature of the trauma can remain unclear, and subsequently, the post-traumatic stress condition of reexperiencing the trauma fails to adequately capture the ways in which "the suffering remains" for those living with cancer.[11]

While the majority of people living with cancer do not meet the criteria for a cancer-related post-traumatic stress disorder diagnosis,[12] many live with one or more of its symptoms. One study of cancer patients shows that about a quarter of patients experience intrusive or distressing thoughts or dreams related to cancer. A sizable minority of people living with cancer also experience emotional numbness or avoidance of thoughts and feelings associated with diagnosis and recurrence; another quarter report hypervigilance and physiological arousal as common; all of these are symptoms of post-traumatic stress.[13] Few studies, however, have yet to limit their focus to a single type of cancer at a specific stage; therefore it remains difficult to compare findings when the types and stages of cancer—as well as treatment protocols and whether patients also have current or past psychiatric illnesses—have yet to be adequately taken into account. To make diagnosis and assessment even more complicated, there is not yet a widely accepted instrument to screen for post-traumatic stress in patients with cancer.[14]

Nevertheless, the studies that have been conducted *do* attest to what researchers call the *chronicity* of cancer-related experiences of trauma—the ongoingness of treatment for the disease along with the risk of recurrence for those whose cancer is not deemed chronic. The chronicity of the condition influences the ongoing character of the post-traumatic stress symptoms experienced by those living with cancer. One study demonstrated that a year after treatment ended for forty-six women with breast cancer, no significant improvement could be documented in symptoms of post-traumatic stress reported by the women in their initial and follow-up interviews. In fact, more than one in ten participants reported an *increase* in symptoms of post-traumatic stress. Even twenty years out from chemotherapy, one in seven women treated for breast cancer continued to experience two or more symptoms of post-traumatic stress that were moderately or extremely bothersome.[15]

Even though trauma's relationship to cancer receives sustained attention within the realm of medical research, only a fraction of people living with cancer who report levels of psychic distress currently receive any type of psychosocial therapy.[16] With estimates of fifteen million new cases of cancer diagnosis to occur in the year 2020,[17] arriving at a better understanding of how the psychic wounds of trauma affect those living with cancer is vital to helping them (us) live with potentially damaging psychosocial effects of the disease, and hence live better, even well.

While important similarities exist between the ways that trauma works in the lives of those who've endured acts of violence and the lives of those who live with life-threatening illness, one key difference between the two is this: rather than being an enemy invasion or threat from the outside, illnesses like cancer are primarily *internal* threats. Augustus Waters, the teen-aged protagonist dying of cancer in John Green's novel *The Fault in Our Stars* wonders out loud, "What am I at war with? My cancer. And what is my cancer? My cancer is me. The tumors are made of me. They're made of me as surely as my brain and my heart are made of me. . . ."[18] That our cancer is "us" creates a distinctive way of experiencing the trauma related to living with this internal reality that threatens to kill us.

"It is the emotional part [of living with cancer] that becomes the greater challenge," admits Rodney, a husband who takes care of his spouse living with advanced-stage cancer.[19] Regardless of whether those who are seriously ill have diagnosable post-traumatic stress, applying the lens of trauma to those living with life-threatening illness deepens our understanding of the range of emotional responses that occur when living with cancer; it opens up more breathing room for those who live with cancer; and the lens of trauma offers those who care for people who are really sick a broader framework in which to offer that care. Sociologist of illness Arthur Frank argues that when those of us who are ill get to tell our stories and have them really listened to, the potential for healing increases.[20] This is especially important work for Christian theologians, clergy, and communities of faith: envisioning what it means to be the body of Christ to and with those who suffer.

As a theologian living with incurable cancer, I've become more aware of how our versions of the Christian story bend toward resolution while the plots of our own lives stubbornly resist it. One of the key insights from trauma studies is that living in the aftermath of traumatic events requires negotiating the ways in which traumatic aftereffects interrupt life in the present. When insights from research on illness-related trauma are placed in conversation with theologians who take other types of trauma research seriously, it becomes possible to contribute to a more expansive telling of the Christian story, one that makes more space—theologically, pastorally, and ecclesially—for the traumatized, particularly those traumatized by serious illness.

What's Ahead

If we move beyond the confines of battle imagery and tidy frameworks of the meaning of illness, what is it that we hear from those who suffer from serious illnesses like cancer? Chapter 1 begins there, listening to cancer stories that expose dimensions of living with illness that make it so difficult to be ill—and to be with those who are ill—places where the anomie related to cancer becomes most insistent and acute. These stories offer glimpses not only into the most unsettling aspects of being sick but also into some ways in which those whose lives are undone by cancer manage to find ways to continue on.

Chapter 2 utilizes recent work in trauma studies to explore in more depth the most unsettling aspects of the cancer stories discussed in chapter 1. These examinations help sharpen our understanding of the distinctive ways in which the ongoingness of illness-related trauma—a trauma that often emerges largely outside networks of moral evil—operates for those who live with it.

Chapter 3 builds on insights of theologians engaging trauma studies to explore those places in the Christian story that make space for expressions of anger, protest, and anguish that come from being seriously ill. Exploring space for illness-related trauma amid the psalms of lament, the story of Job, the god-forsaken Christ on the cross, and Holy Saturday helps expand boundaries of conventional tellings of the Christian story. The chapter focuses on moments in the biblical narrative where movement beyond the bounds of moral framing is glimpsed, where space is created to be in relationship to God amid life-threatening conditions—space that allows room for protest, anguish, trust, and praise.

Listening to some of the ways cancer undoes those who live with it, using the tools from trauma studies to see more fully the suffering that remains for those who are sick, and making more space in the telling of the Christian story for those undone by serious illness all lead to a vision in chapter 4 for what it means to be the church for those who are undone by suffering—particularly the suffering that has no easily identifiable perpetrator. From embodied rituals of lament and healing in worship to forms of care embodied and lived out in and through community, those undone by illness witness an acknowledgment of their suffering and are surrounded in ways that help assuage feelings of despair, even when the anomie remains.

All of this leads, finally, to hope. The concluding chapter explores the ongoing challenges of living with a chronic illness. Turning to Paul's exhortation in 1 Thessalonians 4 that

Christians should grieve not as those who have no hope, I explore the relevance of Paul's vision for ways to affirm the irresolute, not-yet-resurrection time in which we live as also a time of hope for the healing that comes from being able to grieve while also hoping in the more of God's future.

Exploring what it means to be undone by serious illness using the language of trauma, identifying more spacious tellings of the Christian story, and finding images of Christian community that open up more room for the undone all provide, for me, an exercise in hope. It doesn't make sense of my own intimate acquaintance with cancer, but it helps me glimpse a divine future that opens more pathways for living with serious illness in this not-yet-resurrection time. My hope is that it will open up similar pathways for others who live with the death-dealing realities of serious illness.

CHAPTER 1

—————— ∞∞∞ ——————

UNDONE BY CANCER

Cancer stories are everywhere. Family members, neighbors, co-workers, friends, and friends of friends have cancer stories. They regularly appear in the media and on bestseller lists. Most of us can recite the all-too-familiar plotline: the mysterious symptoms and multiple medical tests, the devastating diagnosis and aggressive treatments, the disorienting side effects and the hoped-for-but-not-always-realized remission. We root for happy endings to these stories, participate in them when we can with offers of care and support, and draw inspiration from those who confront their illness with courage and grace.

Cancer stories are everywhere, and we know them well. We know them well not just because they're everywhere but because we're drawn to them out of anticipation for what clues they might offer for negotiating our own present and future. Paul Kalanithi, whose best-selling memoir *When Breath Becomes Air* chronicles his diagnosis and life with stage-IV lung cancer, says this about why he decided to share his own cancer story: "[The reader] can get into these shoes, walk a bit, and say, 'So that's what it looks like from here.' [It's] not the sensationalism of dying, and not exhortations to gather rosebuds, but: Here's what lies up ahead on the road."[1]

All of us know we're going to die — someday. But people who are seriously ill know this acutely. And that perspective nudges us toward compelling cancer stories like Kalanithi's, scanning the terrain for signposts, road maps, and landmarks that help reassure us that making meaning is still possible "up ahead," even when the next leg of the journey includes life-threatening illness.

I used to take in these stories from my residence in the land of the well, but my forced relocation into the land of the ill means that cancer stories look and sound different from the way they did before I got sick. Disruptions in the narrative come into focus. These days I find myself gravitating toward the irresolution that echoes between the well-known chapters. Residency in the land of the ill has made me aware that the cancer-story plotline we think we know often gets streamlined, its rough edges smoothed over.

It's not that cancer stories have completely different plotlines than do stories from the land of the well. As Kalanithi says, it's the up-ahead sightline that's distinctive. The acuteness of the vision threatens well-developed structures of meaning making, of nomos. Atul Gewande, author of *Being Mortal: Medicine and What Matters in the End*, insists that we all know that our bodies will eventually fall apart. Thanks to modern medicine, however, we are living in the midst of a biological revolution regarding expectations of human life. We're thus experiencing a cultural revolution about how we think about the parameters of our mortality.[2]

So when someone is abruptly exiled to the land of the ill, especially in or before the prime of life, an anxious curiosity threatens to overtake our sense of nomos and the accompanying belief that we've got eight or nine decades to live. Especially when illness strikes the young, it compels us to acknowledge that even though so many of us live longer and enjoy healthier lives than those who've gone before, cancer is not yet vanquished, and the possibility of being handed our own personal cancer story is a live possibility.

Arthur Frank, whose work as a sociologist includes investigating the stories we tell one another about illness, says that seriously ill people "need to become storytellers in order to recover the voices that illness and its treatment often take away."[3] People living with cancer tell stories to recover their voices, to better understand their bodies and lives disrupted and rearranged by illness, and to figure out how to continue to live while being persistently susceptible to anomie, that sense of chaos and disorientation that a serious diagnosis can bring. The more the tellers of stories of life with cancer recognize that the particularities of *their own* stories are being heard, the more possible it is for those who are ill to recognize how they might go on amid lives upended by cancer.

As Frank notes, the stories we tell give form to lives that inherently lack form.[4] But giving form to lives shattered by cancer also has its risks. What happens when cancer stories deviate from the plotline we think they should follow? There's pressure in the land of the ill to conform to versions of the cancer story that are palatable, relatable, meaningful, and saturated with hope. There's pressure to downplay the nonsensical, to ignore fissures that redirect the plot. And from the perspective of the land of the well, cancer stories that linger over the anomic plot developments tend to disturb and disorient, leaving the well in a state of uncertainty about how to respond or relate. Danger lurks for both the tellers and the hearers under the influence of streamlined versions of the cancer story.

In order for stories to shape both the tellers and the hearers in life-giving ways, Frank proposes "letting stories breathe," letting them have the first word rather than relying on the versions we think we know.[5] When we really listen to another's experience and empathize with it, that act creates more breathing room in the stories we tell one another about living with serious illness, more space to explore how best to be with those who are sick where they live, move, and have their being. If cancer stories help us learn more about how to live, whether we live in the land of the ill or the land of the well, we need to get more practiced at listening carefully to the *particularities* of different cancer stories. In so doing, we will fine-tune our ability to make more space for the unexpected, irresolute, anomic moments that permeate these stories. When we expand and stretch cancer stories and let them breathe, it becomes more possible to offer the care and support that those in the land of the ill actually need.

Dying at age thirty-seven, less than two years after he was diagnosed with stage-IV lung cancer, Paul Kalanithi did not get to live nearly long enough with his own cancer story. But he left an exquisite testament to his attempt to live fully and sometimes even well with aggressive cancer. A gifted neurosurgical resident at Stanford University, Kalanithi was forced to the sidelines of his practice by invasive, incurable cancer. But with treatment the cancer momentarily receded, and his oncologist recommended that he return to work. Kalanithi reminded her that he was dying. She reminded him that he still had life yet to live.

As a doctor who regularly treated patients with terminal illness, Kalanithi thought that he had developed some sense of what it was like to be seriously ill. "But I'd had no idea how hard it would be," he admits. "I hadn't expected the prospect of facing my own mortality to be so disorienting, so dislocating."[6] Kalanithi struggled to figure out how to continue living when he knew his remaining time would likely be short. He eventually returned to one of the loves of his life—literature—in search of language to help orient him to life on the edge of death. Kalanithi writes about yet another day when he awoke in pain, with no prospects in sight other than eating breakfast. *"I can't go on,* [he] thought, and immediately, its antiphon responded, completing Samuel Beckett's seven words," words he had learned long ago: *I'll go on.* "I got out of bed and took a step forward," he writes, "repeating the phrase over and over: 'I can't go on. I'll go on.'"[7]

The Mantra of those Undone by Cancer

"I can't go on." To experience the world as so anomic as to not want to go on is an experience we all fear. And the fear of meaninglessness propels us toward stories of illness that make sense.

We seek stories that provide explanations for the diagnosis that affirm a nomos, logical explanations that tell us about treatment—especially in our first-world context—that's likely to be effective; stories that testify to the ways in which illness makes possible the emergence of a crystal-clear vision of what's most important in life. Adding a religious gloss to these stories, many believe, is supposed to reinforce that much-desired sense of logic and meaning. Christians often map stories of illness onto a narrative arc that moves from vanquishing the evils of illness to embracing the new life that follows, and in so doing, they crowd out the cries of anomie.

But if theologians and religious leaders are going to tell, ritually enact, and live out versions of the Christian story that make space for the cries of "I can't go on" of those living with serious illness, it is imperative that they listen carefully for those pressure points in stories of illness where "I can't go on" becomes most insistent. What follows is an exercise in paying close attention to the "I can't go on" moments in the stories of those living with cancer. I examine four cancer story lines that challenge conventional, nomic understandings of what it means to live with cancer. Each story line emerges from a first-person accounting of an adult living with cancer. On the one hand, authors of these passages represent a limited sampling of the millions of cancer stories that exist all around us. All of them are well-educated North Americans who have access to quality medical care, commonalities that place them in an elite group. At the same time, their stories serve as pathways into larger conversations about the pressure points in cancer stories that threaten, disrupt, or crowd out meaning.

The first story line focuses on the toll cancer takes on bodies and on how one lives in the world as a body-self. The second chronicles the pressure that those who live with cancer feel to tell positive stories about their illness and how such pressure affects their ability to communicate what it's like to be undone by illness. That cancer diagnoses require renegotiation with the future is the focus of the third story line, and the final section explores how the first three trajectories combine to consistently obstruct attempts to locate nomos when living with serious illness.

While each of the four sections begins with an individual cancer story, additional cancer stories that witness to these particular ways of becoming undone by illness are woven into each section. No two cancer stories are exactly alike, but many of our stories share similar pressure points where—if we pay close attention—cries of "I can't go on" are consistently heard. It is also important to note that these stories are told with little use of secondary literature to interpret or analyze them. Chapter 2 returns to these stories, analyzing and interpreting them using research on illness-related trauma, but the goal in the present chapter is to let these stories breathe so that the occasions for trauma are allowed to rise to the surface.

One last caveat before turning to the "I Can't Go On" story lines: even as the accent in Kalanithi's use of Beckett's phrase is on the experience of becoming undone, that's not all there is to Beckett's phrase, or to any of the cancer stories explored in this chapter. Central to Kalanithi's opting to continue to live is his embrace of the final three words: *I'll go on*. How do those undone by serious illness commit to going on, even amid the unlikelihood of recovery? It is also possible, if we pay close attention, to catch glimpses of "I'll go on" in each of these story lines, even when the anomie continues to disorient and upend. These story lines illustrate well how attempts at restoring nomos are often partial, temporary, and provisional. And still people facing life-threatening challenges choose, against the odds, to go on.

"I Can't Go On" Story Line 1:
No Longer Recognizing Myself

While many of my friends know that I am undergoing treatment for ovarian cancer, very few of them have been told about the intestinal disasters with which I daily contend. But self-censorship gnaws at me. In part, I dwell on Virginia Woolf's lament . . . that her generation was not yet able to tell the truth about the body. Presumably, I am too well educated to be ashamed by a physiological phenomenon beyond my control, but all the

social mores surrounding evacuation and excretion con-
spire to make the ileostomy unspeakable and unspeakably
anxiety-producing.

—Susan Gubar[8]

When she was in her early sixties, Susan Gubar, writer and professor emerita of English and Women's Studies, was diagnosed with
advanced-stage ovarian cancer, a cancer rarely detected until it's
advanced and—more often than not—terminal. Ovarian-cancer
stories are among the least-well-known cancer stories, counting
for just 3 percent of cancers diagnosed in U.S. women, but coming in fifth as the leading cause of cancer-related deaths for those
same women.[9] While survival rates for other cancers have been
on a steady march of improvement, rates of survival for ovarian
cancer have remained stable since the 1970s.

Some of the most familiar and most feared elements of the
cancer story are the bodily symptoms that show up and register
the possibility that something is wrong. A lump in the breast, an
atypical-looking mole, a cough that refuses to go away—all can
be potential indications of cancer. But the plots of cancer stories
become more complicated when cancer fails to manifest itself
through clear and predictable signs. The ovarian-cancer story
has just this type of plotline. The symptoms—bloating, fatigue,
indigestion, constipation—masquerade, Gubar wryly notes, as
"the inevitabilities of middle age." This means that the signs are
frequently misunderstood, and with no reliable screening, ovarian cancer is free to grow and spread. Gubar's own advanced-
stage diagnosis quickly propelled her into a grueling surgery
that wreaked havoc not just on her body but also on her well-
honed sense of self.

The title of her cancer story, *Memoir of a Debulked Woman*, references the standard treatment for ovarian cancer: a surgical
debulking, where attempts are made to remove as much of the
cancer as possible, including parts of organs where malignancy
exists. The body is sliced open from the navel to pubic bone,
and surgeons work for hours to remove as much cancer as possible. Even though she had access to high-quality medical care,

Gubar's own debulking was deemed "suboptimal" because of the surgeons' inability to remove all of the lesions, leaving her with increased risk of recurrence.

During the operation, Gubar's colon was perforated, resulting in multiple postsurgery problems, including persistent accumulation of fluid, repeated infections, dreadful drains, and eventually, an ileostomy, a procedure that opens up the abdominal wall in order to bring the ileum (the lowest part of the small intestine) out onto the surface of the skin. The ileostomy left Gubar severely limited in what she could eat, as well as with a digestive process that gets rid of her body's waste through the stoma (an opening made in the abdomen) and into a pouch attached to the skin.

Listening for the pressure points in cancer stories where cries of "I can't go on" emerge begins by taking time to appreciate the reality that cancer begins *in and with the body*. In every type of cancer, there's a breakdown of one or more cell-growth control systems. Some of the body's cells begin to divide without stopping and spread to surrounding tissue. Whether it travels through the bloodstream or prompts the creation of tumors, cancer disrupts the body's ability to function. But it's not only the cancer that makes life-threatening changes to the body it inhabits, it is also the treating of the cancer, that in attempting to halt the disease often brings further pain and harm. A less-appreciated dimension of the cancer-story plot is how such disruption to the body affects the self-understanding of someone used to living in the world with a functioning, able body. Arthur Frank puts it this way: "Illness is a story about moving from a comfortable body to one that forces me to ask: What's happening to me? Not it, but *me*."[10]

In the excerpt from her cancer story quoted above, Gubar calls living in the aftermath of her suboptimal debulking and ileostomy not just "unspeakable" but also "unspeakably anxiety-producing." She searches mostly in vain for writings by other women with ovarian cancer who bear witness to life after ileostomy—or its close cousin, the colostomy—to help her find language and any accompanying sense of nomos in relation to continuing to live with a debulked body alongside a diagnosis of incurable cancer. In the pages of her memoir, Gubar struggles to overcome the self-censorship she experiences in face-to-face conversations with those close to her by offering detailed written accounts of what living with the ileostomy looks like, smells like, and acts like. She tops off these cringe-worthy descriptions with passages from the few women she managed to discover who had survived debulking and digestive rerouting and wrote about it. "I detested myself," one confessed. Another wrote, "It's horrible. I'd rather be dead."[11]

Gubar has now lived with ovarian cancer for almost a decade, and part of letting her story breathe involves paying attention to how and why she's been able to go on, even with a debulked body. But first it is important to linger a bit longer in this space of the self that feels alienated from the body and the toll it takes on the person forced to negotiate what it means to live with a body of proliferating cancerous cells and medicines that kill healthy and cancerous cells alike. Gubar suggests that part of what makes finding language up to the task of capturing the self/body renegotiation so difficult is that the cancerous cells are not actually invaders but one's own cells and organs gone awry. Therefore, cancer's own working within the body helps generate an experience of exile from the self.

"I don't recognize my body," writes now-deceased Carrie Host, who at age thirty-nine was diagnosed with and treated for metastatic carcinoid cancer, a rare, slow-growing cancer that, like ovarian cancer, is typically not detected until it is advanced and life-threatening.[12] Similar to Gubar's story, the plotline of Host's story also moves at frightening speed toward a debilitating surgery that leaves her spending most of her time in a hospital room, in bed, or on the family-room couch, unable to fulfill the parental roles she had taken great pleasure in doing before she got sick.

"I'm trapped in a body that won't do what I tell it to do," Host admits rather incredulously as she's forced to watch her family's world continue on without her, especially the care of her youngest son who was less than a year old at the time of her diagnosis. Like Gubar, Host doesn't shy away from writing about the mind-numbing pain cancer and its treatments level against her body. Even more, however, Host is intent on communicating the challenges she experiences in coming to terms with her relationship to her own depleted body and her relationship to others through this body so compromised by cancer and its treatment. It's the having "to stand by like a stranger in [her] own life"[13] that leads Host to wonder how she'll go on.

Inhabiting a body with cancer is not the only source of exilic experience in cancer stories; as is the case with Gubar, it is also the removal of body parts that precipitates a wandering in an identity wilderness. After her diagnosis with breast cancer and subsequent mastectomy, African American writer and activist Audre Lorde attempts to come to terms with what having breast cancer means. While still in the hospital, Lorde writes, "I want to write of the pain I am feeling right now, of the lukewarm tears that will not stop coming into my eyes—for what? For my lost breast? For the lost me? And which me was that again anyway? For the death I don't know how to postpone? Or how to meet elegantly?"[14] Lorde searches for words spacious enough to hold her lament, sadness, and feelings of anomie. She mourns her amputated breast, especially when she is confronted with the realization of the role it played in her understanding of herself as a woman.

Lorde also describes the excruciating physical pain of having her breast surgically removed—of the draining tubes, the numbness. But even as she recovers from the physical pain of the surgery, months later she continues to reflect on how the amputation of this tangible sign of womanhood takes its toll of her self-understanding:

> I seem to move so much more slowly now these days. It is as if I cannot do the simplest thing, as if nothing at all is done without a decision, and every decision is so crucial. Yet I feel strong and able in general, and only sometimes do I touch that battered place where I am totally inadequate to anything I most wish to accomplish. To put it another way, I feel always tender in the wrong places.[15]

The disruption cancer and its treatment create in Lorde's understanding of herself as a body-self is poignantly captured by her question "How do I live with myself one-breasted? What posture do I take, literally, with my physical self?"[16] Her disorientation is palpable. Losing a breast challenges Lorde's relationship to herself as a female body. She's unsure of how to interact with the world in which she was formerly a two-breasted woman.

The way Gubar tells the story, it's the demands of her altered, cancer-ridden body that prevent her from being the person she previously knew herself to be. Life after surgery requires having a bathroom in sight at all times and leaves little mental space for thoughts beyond stool softeners. She admits, "It's the tyranny of the body—the treachery of the body—[that] comes into focus: how the sick or dysfunctional body trumps not only mind and heart but also volition or will. I no longer 'have' or 'relate to' a body. This injured body rules me."[17]

Glimpses of "I'll Go On": Not Alone in My Suffering

How, then, does Gubar's cancer story move from her writing about other debulked women who wish they were dead to watching—after a brief year of remission—"with incredulity, [her] revitalized self [urge] the diseased person [she] had been pronounced to be to undertake another round of treatments that would haul [her] back into the torpor"? What leads her to opt for a return to the chemicals that render her existence a "life-in-death"?[18]

Gubar receives news of the cancer's recurrence while she's training to be a volunteer at the local hospice center in her neighborhood. From the perspective of hospice care, agreeing to more chemotherapy is considered a "curative" rather than "palliative" approach to care, even though in Gubar's case, chemo is not able to cure the cancer, only, *possibly*, to keep it contained a while longer. And yet, even though no cure exists, Gubar admits, "The thought of allowing the cancer to colonize my kidneys, intestines, and life horrifies me." Therefore, she opts for more chemotherapy.[19] Even though her life is more reclusive than she ever envisioned it would or could be, Gubar still savors her "usual pleasures" of reading, writing, and loving. And she's desperate to hold on to that life as long as she can.

Round 2 of chemo bludgeons her spirit and besets her body with another round of infections. Her oncologists urge her toward another abdominal surgery, and after much more endurance of awfulness—the pain, the compromised living—Gubar finds herself, stunningly, in a second remission. While she is undergoing a whirlwind of additional treatments, Gubar meets with yet another oncologist, who says to her, "The fact that you had a suboptimal debulking does not make you a suboptimal person!" Gubar is initially outraged that a doctor would say such a thing, out loud, to a debulked woman. Later, however, Gubar wonders whether enduring life with incurable ovarian cancer has, in fact, made her a suboptimal person.

The question looms large when, in the final days of the year of the cancer's recurrence, Gubar's husband and a friend together ask about her fondest memory of the past year. Gubar admits that the recurrence and the subsequent treatment have colonized her mind, leaving her at a loss to conjure up any "good" memories of the year. Gubar has to rely on her friend's recollection of a joyous gathering of Gubar's graduate students the previous spring and her husband's recounting of "an enchanted get-together" of extended family the previous summer. It unnerves her to realize that memories of sun-soaked joy were squeezed out of her mind by the domineering presence of cancer and all that it demanded from her.

But in the final two pages of her memoir, Gubar describes what researching, reading, and writing about her and others' cancer stories did for her during the worst days of her illness: "Reading and writing about cancer cast a lifeline between me and people whose honesty about mortal encounters mitigated my fearful loneliness and thereby steadied me."[20] Over the past several years, Gubar has continued writing about living with cancer on a *New York Times* blog. In 2016, Gubar released another book,

Reading and Writing Cancer: How Words Heal,[21] where she reflects on the power of sharing our cancer stories with a network of witnesses. Throughout the book, she weaves reflections on journeying with cancer into the larger narrative of life through integration of insights from novels, plays, film, poetry, and paintings, pushing at the parameters of cancer stories and highlighting their intersections with other stories of our mortality.

Finding companionship in others' stories of living with their own "unspeakable" versions of illness—along with writing her own—helps Gubar envision what it's like to continue to live when you're really sick. But just as much, it's the "ongoing intimacy with family and friends accustomed to [her] perpetual reversals" that helps her continue on. Her husband, daughters, and close friends offer steady support through the daily anomic challenges of living with incurable cancer.

"I Can't Go On" Story Line 2:
The Tyranny of the Positive Cancer Story

In the mainstream of breast cancer culture, there is very little anger, no mention of possible environmental causes, and few comments about the fact that, in all but the more advanced, metastasized cases, it is the "treatments," not the disease, that cause the immediate illness and pain. In fact, the overall tone is almost universally upbeat. The Breast Friends Web site, for example, featured a series of inspirational quotes: "Don't cry over anything that can't cry over you," "I can't stop the birds of sorrow from circling my head, but I can stop them from building a nest in my hair." . . . Positive thinking seems to be mandatory in the breast cancer world, to the point that unhappiness requires a kind of apology.

—Barbara Ehrenreich[22]

It was difficult for writer Barbara Ehrenreich to come to terms with the biopsy result that revealed she had breast cancer. She had no family history of the disease; she ranked low on other typical indicators; and at age fifty-nine she was in excellent overall health. Despite the demographic unlikelihood of getting the disease, she found herself with a cancerous tumor in her breast and an involuntary initiation into the breast-cancer story of intensive chemotherapy and subsequent side effects of the physical and more-than-physical kind.

To help prepare for the not-yet-written chapters in her own cancer story, Ehrenreich sought out stories of other women living with breast cancer. Given that there are over 300,000 women diagnosed with breast cancer each year in the United States alone,[23] it didn't take long to find them—lots and lots of them. Ehrenreich immersed herself in these stories to the point of acquiring a "panicky fascination" about all that could go wrong with treatment and about how the diagnosis could be— or could grow to be—much worse than her current treatable version of the disease. The more she let herself be worked on by these many versions of the breast-cancer story the more isolated she felt. Few subplots left room for anger over getting breast cancer, and it was only a rare story line that seemed to devote adequate space to the sadness, the grief, and the unrelenting physical pain. Ehrenreich found herself, time and time again, face-to-face with a narrative arc that stubbornly, relentlessly, bent toward positivity.

As her words above illustrate, Ehrenreich encounters multiple variations of the breast-cancer story that frame life with cancer as an opportunity to do better, be better. There are stories admitting that the year of treatment for breast cancer was the hardest of all years, only to be followed up with the emphatic conclusion that it was also the most rewarding of years. The real story, these survivors testify, is not the cancer story per se. The *real* story is what the cancer story makes possible: opportunities to get rid of old baggage, repair frayed relationships, make new friends, and take better care of one's body and spirit.

While Ehrenreich's own body and spirit were being put through the grueling paces of hair loss, nausea, and other chemotherapeutic unpleasantries, she writes about being worked on by breast-cancer story lines that depict these experiences as meaningfully character building, edifying, and redemptive. The main characters of the breast-cancer story witnessed to how treatment for breast cancer left them stronger and happier than ever before. Life after cancer becomes infused with meaning that was lacking in life before cancer.

Even as she was confronted with a tyranny of positivity, Ehrenreich held out hope that stories about complaints over lost time or shattered views of one's body had to be out there somewhere. She reasoned that there had to be women (and men) who were willing to go on record expressing grief over things like arm strength being permanently compromised by removal of lymph nodes. But even when a cancer story made a bit of space for acknowledging the considerable physical and emotional pain or lasting disfigurement — or more rarely, for the possibility that cancer can lead to premature death — Ehrenreich was dismayed to discover that such indulgences are invariably followed by a "but" that routinely includes a realization that cancer ultimately leads to more happiness and the possibility of becoming a new and better self.

Ehrenreich traces the narrative arc of positivity that stretches as far as bestowing on cancer the role of "gift" in the lives of those who get diagnosed with it. A cancer diagnosis, according to the cancer-as-gift story line, opens up new, nomic ways of living that would not have been possible without cancer. There is often a theological overlay for this plot development as well. In order for cancer to be a gift, there needs to be a Giver, a path that often leads to the Divine. God gives the gift of cancer so that the recipient might appreciate life anew and live into her full God-given potential. For all who believe that the Divine is involved in the stories of our lives (Ehrenreich does not count herself among this group), the question of God's role in illness remains an insistent one. As Ehrenreich suggests, believing that God is part of your story often translates into believing in God's direct involvement in the cancer.

Shortly after thirty-five-year-old religion professor Kate Bowler was diagnosed with an aggressive form of colon cancer, a neighbor suggested to her husband that everything — even his wife's cancer—happens for a reason. Bowler's husband pressed the neighbor to explain what the reason might be for his wife's virtual death sentence, a request the neighbor was unprepared to answer. In her reflection over this exchange between her husband and the neighbor, Bowler acknowledges the strong desire for many people of faith to fit a sudden, life-threatening diagnosis into a nomic structure. "She wanted some kind of order behind this chaos," Bowler writes. "Because the opposite of [being blessed by God] is leaving a husband and toddler behind, and people can't quite let themselves say it: 'Wow. That's awful.' There has to be a reason, because without one we are left as helpless and possibly as unlucky as everyone else."[24] When cancer is seen as a gift given by the Divine, one is neither helpless nor unlucky. One is given an opportunity to become a better, God-ordained self, to come through a challenging experience stronger and more resilient than you were before.

Ehrenreich makes it her mission to resist the tyranny of the positive breast-cancer story, whether God is part of the plot or not. Because her own version of the cancer story includes multiple inhalations of anger, grief, and nausea, she takes a risk and publicly protests our collective obsession with positive cancer stories. Her first such forum for pushing back is an online breast-cancer message board. In her entry titled "Angry," Ehrenreich chronicles her experiences with the debilitating effects of chemo, challenges with insurance companies, suspicions about environmental contributors to this cancer that afflicts hundreds of thousands of women, and, to top it off, a "daring" critique of "sappy pink ribbons."[25] A couple of women offer encouragement regarding her challenges surrounding adequate insurance coverage. But most women who respond to Ehrenreich's post rebuke her for refusing to frame her breast-cancer story in positive, meaningful terms. She is called out for her "bad attitude," and encouraged to redirect her energies toward a more peaceful, happy existence. Fellow breast-cancer sufferers recommend therapy and counsel her to fight the temptation to be bitter about the cancer.[26]

Despite the pressure to tell a positive, uplifting cancer story, Ehrenreich insists on more breathing room, determined to make space for anomic expressions like Bowler's about the chaotic awfulness of living with cancer. She continues her search for alternative plotlines that challenge the effervescent "breast-cancer cleanse made me whole" story line. This search eventually results in her book chapter "Smile or Die: The Bright Side of Cancer." Here she describes how these alternative versions of the breast-cancer story are being squeezed out by the prevalence of positivity. Her research uncovers stories of women being kicked out of breast-cancer support groups when their cancer metastasizes because the group cannot handle someone who will never become a "survivor"[27] and of women who dare to tell not-so-positive versions of their cancer stories and are compelled to apologize for deviating from the plot.

Ehrenreich's sustained reflection on the pressure to tell a positive cancer story makes visible some of the potential dangers of the insistence on striving toward nomos in prominent, public versions of the cancer story. When she struggles with how to go on amid devastating physical and mental effects of having and being treated for cancer, her attempts are met with recommendations that she keep those feelings to herself.

Glimpses of "I'll Go On": Telling Realistic Cancer Stories

What does "going on" look like in the face of relentless pressure to be positive about life with cancer? According to Ehrenreich, the alternative to positive thinking is not despair. Negative thinking—imagining the worst possible outcome for every situation—carries with it its own set of dangers. To always assume the worst, she argues, is simply another problematic way of striving for nomos. The alternative to both positive and negative thinking is "to get outside of ourselves," Ehrenreich proposes, and understand the world as full of both danger and opportunity—as presenting chances at happiness as well as the certainty of death.[28]

When it comes to telling cancer stories, then, it's the realistic versions she's after, the ones that make space for the anomie and the awfulness. Ehrenreich is also interested in making space for the scientific research connected to cancer and attitude. She points to studies that challenge conventional wisdom that says cancer patients' attitudes affect the outcome of their cancer. In a previous life, Ehrenreich earned a doctorate in cell immunology, making her conversant with scientific plotlines of the cancer story. She rehearses how what we know scientifically about the immune system makes it hard to claim that positive thinking boosts the immune system, which in turn improves the body's ability to fight cancerous cells. The story of the immune system is that it takes on intruders within the body, but cancer cells—which are the body's own cells set to an abnormal duplication cycle—are not themselves intruders. While one of the most promising recent developments for treating cancer is immunotherapy, the training of one's immune system to identify and go after cancer cells, this medical approach differs from the idea that positive thinking will stimulate the immune system.

Ehrenreich draws on the work of health psychologist Penelope Schofield and her study that showed no benefits of an optimistic attitude among lung-cancer patients. Based on the study's conclusions, Schofield argues,

> We should question whether it is valuable to encourage optimism if it results in the patient concealing his or her distress in the misguided belief that this will afford survival benefits. . . . If a patient feels generally pessimistic . . . it is important to acknowledge these feelings as valid and acceptable.[29]

Ehrenreich rightly points out that the "Attitude Is Everything" approach to living with cancer is yet another variation on the positive cancer story. Especially in stories where there's a desperate need for an infusion of hope, the temptation to encourage the one with cancer to be positive, to refuse to give up, can be almost impossible to resist. In striving for nomos and against the anomic pressures of living with cancer, we trust that it must be possible to have some control over whatever cancer story comes our way.

But Ehrenreich is sensitive to the perniciousness of the "It's All Attitude" plotline. While there's evidence that certain behaviors—smoking, lack of exercise, eating vast amounts of fast food—increase the risk of cancer and other health issues, for a sizable number of us who get cancer, direct causes—even significant contributing factors—are often elusive. The lack of any clear cause of the cancer points in an anomic direction, a direction few of us want to look.

In life before my own cancer diagnosis, I worked hard at living a healthy life. I slept eight hours a night, exercised multiple times a week, ate a vegetarian diet—all "good choices" that are commonly understood as enabling a long and healthy life. But getting knocked down with life-threatening cancer in my early forties issued a steep challenge to my nomic conviction that in terms of health, we always reap what we sow. Residing in the land of the ill these past nine years has made me more aware of how many of us are wedded to this conviction that we control our health.

"The doctors told her it's 90 percent attitude," a friend told me brightly after his wife's latest trip to the oncology clinic. I winced involuntarily, as if my stomach had just run into someone's fist. His wife had stage-IV cancer and lousy odds of living long with the disease. As his breath of hope hung in the air, I weighed whether or not to point out to my friend the alternative version of the "Attitude Is [Almost] Everything" cancer story. The version where his wife's health deteriorates and her worsening condition—because it's 90 percent based on attitude—becomes 90 percent her fault. Given my own encounters with pressure to believe that we control how well we do with our version of the cancer story, I opted to let the "Attitude Is Everything" cancer story breathe a bit. "But what if—*God forbids*—she doesn't get better?" I croaked. "Surely we won't want to conclude that her attitude is mostly responsible for a worsening condition?"

It can be difficult to tell a not-so-positive, attitude-is-not-everything version of the cancer story, but telling a realistic cancer story includes making room to resist tidy connections between attitude and one's ability to live long or well with life-threatening diseases like cancer. Going beyond the conventional cancer story line, as Ehrenreich does, opens up space for those living with cancer to tell their own stories and have them heard. By insisting on more realistic versions of the cancer story, we can prevent exhortations to think positively from becoming "an additional burden to an already devastated patient."[30]

In discussing the telling of realistic cancer stories, Ehrenreich also wades into the contested waters of what language should be used to talk about those of us living with cancer. She makes the case for using words like "victims" or "patients" when talking about those of us who live with cancer. She points out that for activists in the AIDS movement (a movement that has heavily influenced breast-cancer activism), words like "patient" and "victim" have been deemed "too inactive" to attribute to those who are battling breast cancer. Instead those living with breast cancer get verbs: those in the midst of treatments are described as "battling" or "fighting" (often "bravely" or "fiercely").[31] These verbs often accompany the "survivor" story line where the protagonist valiantly wins her battle. And those with particularly lousy prognoses risk being excluded from support groups because survivor language is not spacious enough for them as well.

While Ehrenreich resists military images that talk of fighting cancer, her preference to be called a "victim" of cancer does not necessarily move her beyond military metaphors. She chooses the word intentionally, hoping that more consideration will be given to the *moral* dimensions of the breast-cancer story, particularly regarding how environmental factors contribute to the high rates of the disease among U.S. women. Even though the influence of environmental factors continues to be debated,[32] "victim" imagery can remind us that cancer does not always remain distant from considerations of justice. At the same time, to opt for "victim" as a primary designation of what it means to live with cancer risks downplaying the agency those of us who are ill have in choosing how to respond to our illness.

Susan Gubar also struggles with what language to use to talk about those of us who live with cancer. Like Ehrenreich, she rejects "survivor" language: "For years I have resisted the pervasive tag 'cancer survivor' because it erases or demeans patients who do not or suspect they cannot survive the disease," Gubar writes. What, then, to put in its place? Gubar reviews multiple options, from person living with cancer (PLC) to deceased queer theorist Eve Sedgwick's preferred self-description for her attempts to continue living with metastatic breast cancer: "undead."[33]

Realistic language for realistic cancer stories can help give voice to the anomie brought on by being given one's very own cancer story. But for many authors of cancer stories, the search for adequate language continues, often largely eclipsed by dominant, positive, nomic versions of the stories.

"I Can't Go On" Story Line 3:
Foreclosures of the Future

My doctors were delighted at my body's response to the transplant, and I was giving thanks to God. . . . But to my own surprise, much of my deepest grieving came after this good news. . . . My life would never be the same — I would receive low-dose chemo for as long as my remissions last and frequent cancer tests "until" it returns. When it returns, I will need more intensive treatments. . . . As I thought about returning to my "normal life," I felt more alienated than ever. How was I to respond to ordinary questions like "How are you?" and "How have you been?" How was I to look toward the future — for my family, for my vocation? "My eye grows dim through sorrow. Every day I call on you, O Lord; I spread out my hands to you" (Ps. 88.9). . . . The good news about my transplant didn't take [the] fear away.

—J. Todd Billings[34]

Even though he expected the news to be bad, thirty-nine-year-old seminary professor Todd Billings was unprepared for just how bad it would be. A second meeting with the oncologist confirmed that his cancer story would develop along the plotline of the worst of the options originally laid out for him. He had active multiple myeloma, the cancer where plasma cells overproduce in the bone marrow and crowd out the necessary variation of blood cells. By the time the oncologist delivered the devastating news, Billings's plasma levels were over five times what they're supposed to be, and the cancer had already damaged his skull, arm, and hip. "There's no doubt about the diagnosis," the oncologist confirmed.

"I needed words to pray—I needed a language for my life with God in this moment," Billings writes in his theological memoir *Rejoicing in Lament: Wrestling with Incurable Cancer and Life in Christ*.[35] Throughout the telling of his story, Billings repeatedly testifies to the difficulty of finding language that creates enough room for meaning making about his life with cancer, not to mention his life with God. Resolute in his claim that his life story is but one story line within the larger and more significant narrative of God's story, Billings nevertheless pushes back against the conclusion that just because his story unfolds within the parameters of God's story means that it always makes sense. "God's story is bigger than my cancer story, period," he writes. Yet from the earliest days of his diagnosis, Billings senses that his "unfolding cancer story was not to be denied or repressed because of God's story, either. The news felt like a heavy burden."[36]

Sudden expulsion from the land of the well followed by forced relocation in the land of the ill produces an anomic disorientation that's difficult to describe, much less accept. In my own cancer story, it took being weaned off opioids before the seriousness of my own condition began to sink in. Once I was able to comprehend some of the consequences likely to accompany my story line of advanced-stage, incurable cancer, I was visited repeatedly by a vision of giving back my diagnosis:

I would walk up to the desk at the clinic, clear my throat, and insist, politely yet firmly, that I was ready to give back my diagnosis. I had tried the cancer on for size, and unfortunately, it didn't fit my lifestyle. I would hand the "Stage

IV Cancer" file back to the surprised-yet-unprotesting receptionist at the oncology clinic, and she would nod her head solemnly and take the file from me. Then I would march out of the clinic and back into life as it used to be.[37]

Getting one's mind around what life *with* cancer will look like often seems like an impossible task because the threat to whatever nomos was there before is so strong. On the opening page of *Rejoicing in Lament*, Billings describes the fog that set in for several weeks after receiving his diagnosis. The future — which had seemed so expansive just weeks before — narrowed precipitously. How would it be possible to face these new days crowded with cancer? At the heart of Billings's cancer story is his perpetual wrestling with how to hold his belief in divine providence, the affirmation that the universe is under the care and governance of God, alongside the experiences of terror, fear, and uncertainty that fill his cancer-story plotline. One of the most significant ways this gets worked out is through his wrestling with prayer. He and the Christian communities of which he is a part profess strong belief in the power of prayer. Yet Billings admits he can't fully endorse prayers for him that petition God for "complete healing" or a "cure."

His resistance comes in part from the way his ears ring with the oncologist's declaration that his type of cancer is incurable, and even though remission is possible, the cancer "*will* come back."[38] Billings believes that God can and does heal, but he's also well aware that God's story includes those who are not healed of their sufferings in this life. Perhaps because of his keen awareness of all those lives cut short by cancer, Billings questions whether God owes him — or any of us — a long life. He expresses his frustration with what he calls "the impatience of these prayers" that aim at complete healing and stem from what feels to him like an "impatience that seems to diminish the material, embodied nature of my life as a creature."[39]

Billings also gives voice to the anguish of those of us whose cancer diagnosis comes when we're still parents of young children, where the lament is most acute when we're confronted with a future that includes our children losing a parent at a young age. To have life threatened in the middle years, years often spent raising children, is cause for deep lament.[40] Like the other cancer story lines explored in this chapter, Billings's story is rife with discussions of the "daily, bodily reminders of the current 'reign of death'" brought to him by cancer.[41] To then be told by other well-meaning Christians that this reign of death is part of God's perfect plan feels to him like a minimizing of his pain and a lack of appreciation for the seriousness of his diagnosis. This theologian who trains future pastors has dedicated his vocation to working out claims like "God is good"; but life with cancer, he confesses, can leave him "too weary and weak to trust that the new creation is coming." Sometimes, he breathes, "I'm tired of hoping."[42]

Billings's aching confessions—about the toll cancer takes on his ability to actively embrace the story of faith that's long been his—challenge conventional understandings of how people of faith should respond when suffering comes their way. The cancer story threatens to siphon off his ability to trust and hope in the future, even when he believes that the future belongs to God. The reign of cancer threatens the sense of nomos that people of faith feel they need to hold on to, even in times where a sense of meaninglessness is seeping in from all sides.

In attempts to stem the aggressive tide of his cancer, Billings undergoes a stem-cell transplant that requires several weeks of hospitalization and high-dosage chemotherapy followed by weeks in a sterile cancer lodge. Tests are run after weeks of recovery, and Billings is told that "engraftment"—the process whereby stem cells start to produce new blood cells—is taking place in his bone marrow. This means the procedure was a successful one. It is welcome news, and Billings gives thanks to God. Yet it is precisely at the point where a future of more life is plotted onto his story line that he experiences alienation, grief, and fear more acutely than at any other time since his diagnosis.

Why does good news of effective treatment drag Billings closer to "I can't go on" than anything he had encountered thus far in his cancer story? The exacting nature of the treatments certainly contributes to his inability to imagine what it will take to "go on." He chronicles the overwhelming levels of fatigue he experiences for months following the transplant. His ability to do everyday tasks is severely compromised—every day. Added to that is the isolation that haunts him in the aftermath of the transplant: for two months his compromised immune system prevents him from entering any public space for fear of infection. Other than his immediate family and a very occasional (perfectly healthy) visitor—where he rarely is able to locate words to express how he is doing—he is cut off from daily physical connections that remind him he's part of the land of the living.

Perhaps the most harrowing reality accompanying him at this time is the knowledge that two of his friends' cancer stories are moving away from treatment toward palliative care, toward dying and then to death, just as his story moves toward remission. "But for what?" he laments. "To wait around for this to happen to me, just as it happened to my friends?"[43] While the notes and phone calls accumulate, each of them filled with expressions of joy over his good news, Billings slips more deeply into grief. He struggles to come to terms with his seemingly mismatched response to traversing through the valley of the shadow and getting to return to his life: a "new normal," as they say. "But there was nothing 'normal' about it," writes Billings. "It felt like a new place of isolation, a new place of being misunderstood, a new place of living in fear."[44]

Glimpses of "I'll Go On": Making Space for Lament

Again and again Billings searches for words up to the task of communicating the disorientation and grief brought on by the fading of a once-bright future into a persistent fog of incurable illness and an ever-sick body. Similarly, writer Carrie Host admits that in wrestling with the terms of her own diagnosis, "Words, which I considered my closest companions, have turned on me."[45] Billings's search for adequate words leads him to the

Psalms, particularly to the ones that have to do with lament. In the crucible of wrestling with how to locate his cancer story within the larger truth of God's story, Billings comes to understand in an intimately personal way that lament doesn't just make space for grief and sorrow—it makes space for protest as well.

> O LORD, heal me, for my bones are shaking with terror.
> My soul also is struck with terror,
>> while you, O LORD—how long?
> Turn, O LORD, save my life;
>> deliver me for the sake of your steadfast love.
>
> (Ps. 6:2–4)

References to lament psalms like this one grace the pages of *Rejoicing in Lament*. Their cadence helps hold Billings's sorrow, his grief, and his attempts to trust in God's deliverance. Billings finds lament and protest in the New Testament as well, highlighting the "radical nature of the Christian faith" residing in the line of the Lord's Prayer that bids, "Thy kingdom come, on earth as it is in heaven," a protest to all the ways that life on earth fails to resemble the reign of God.[46] Meditating on lament psalms and the Lord's Prayer leads Billings to Jesus and Jesus' own lamentation in God's story. "Death and dying are included—not excluded—in the story of God," Billings confirms. The good news of the gospel is big enough to incorporate not just our life but, just as importantly, our death.

Glimpsing how to go on through attending to the bigger story of God, Billings comes to accept that it is not his job to write the last chapter of his life. Quoting theologian John Thompson, Billings concludes, " 'It's not your job to make sense of everything. . . . Let God gather up the fragments. Let God finish the story.' "[47] Even though his own story constantly courts anomie, Billings finds comfort in trusting that a nomos exists within God's story. Even when he cannot himself grasp it, he trusts it is there.

As much of Billings's story reflects the intensely individual and isolating nature of living with serious illness, he also gestures toward the indispensability of the support he and his family receive from church and seminary communities. His honest assessment of the difficulty he has with some of the prayers uttered on his behalf does not diminish his appreciation of the reality that he doesn't pray alone. When strength to pray eludes him, others are praying on his behalf. Communal support has been "essential," he says, even as it has been, at times, part of the struggle.[48]

"I Can't Go On" Story Line 4: The Hard Times Make Us . . .

Seven years of cancer have certainly exposed me to wider and more searing notions of suffering (and not only my own), but I'm not sure I'm any more enlightened about what suffering means — or even, in the midst of it, when pain has obliterated my brain, *that* it means. Is this a moral failure or mystical fulfillment? Is it an achievement to reach a point at which I trust that the meaning, which I do not feel, is there, a condition that elsewhere in this book I have called faith? Or should I reach the end of an effort like this, having felt acutely the end of a life like mine . . . with more certainty, more assurance that I am loved by God, some freedom from these cracks that open in my brain, rifts splitting right down to the bright abyss that is, finally, devoid of any meaning but the one I give it?
— Christian Wiman[49]

In the afternoon of his thirty-ninth birthday, less than a year after his wedding day, poet Christian Wiman was diagnosed with a rare form of blood cancer. It's as "rare as it is mysterious," killing some people quickly while others live without symptoms for decades.[50] The cancer's mysterious behavior leaves oncologists unwilling to offer him any kind of prognosis for the future. Wiman describes how everything shifted the moment he learned of his diagnosis. "I can still feel how far away everything—the people walking on the stress beyond the window, the books on the shelf, my wife smiling up at me in the moment before I told her—suddenly seemed." He's confronted with the realization that no small part of his enjoyment of his life thus far had been fueled by an unconscious assumption that it would all continue. Until the reality of our own death is thrust upon us, Wiman acknowledges, ". . . we live in a land where only other people die."[51]

In ways wrenchingly similar to the other cancer stories breathing in this chapter, Wiman allows readers glimpses into the pain brought on by his cancer and its attendant treatments. Even a botched bone-marrow biopsy did not prepare him for the worst of the pain, a time when the cancer took over his bone marrow and inflamed his bones, making them feel like they would burst. "Bones don't like to stretch," a doctor says out loud what his body already knew. The pain was dull and devouring, and even after taking all the pain medicine he could "without dying," he spent his days on the couch, praying more to the pain than to God that it would ease up, that he would be able to breathe without wanting to die. "It islands you," Wiman says of the pain. "You sit there in your little skeletal constriction of self—of disappearing self—watching everyone you love, however steadfastly they may remain by your side, drift farther and farther away."[52]

In his struggle to tell his own cancer story, Wiman searches for a path between resignation to this life of pain that permits only anomie and alienation, and resistance to letting cancer fully determine how he makes his way. He grew up inside a Christianity that made little room for uncertainty, ambiguity, or anomie. Possessed by a poetic sensibility steeped in questions and doubt, Wiman left the faith of his childhood, only to return to church—and eventually, to a renewed sense of faith—around the time of his diagnosis. In his book *My Bright Abyss: Meditations of a Modern Believer*, Wiman proposes an understanding of faith and of God that dances on the edges of incomprehension.

"To say that one must live in uncertainty doesn't begin to get at the tenuous, precarious nature of faith," Wiman writes. "The minute you begin to speak with certitude about God, he is gone."[53] Wiman challenges the conventional view that living a life of faith, especially when times are good, means that life and faith are experienced as fundamentally nomic. Immersed in a world of poetry that witnesses to the persistent eclipse of clarity by questioning and indecision, Wiman insists that to be human is to live without intellectual coherence, in a space where ultimate meaning remains just out of reach.[54] Wiman has long occupied a space where meaning is up for debate, but that his life has had to make room for cancer means that he breathes in T. S. Eliot's "And the time of death is every moment"[55] differently than he did before life with cancer. It's qualitatively different, Wiman admits, to contemplate this line when "massive unmetaphorical pain goes crawling through your bones, when fear—goddamn fear, you can't get rid of it—ices your spine."[56] While Wiman attests to God's giving him courage during previous trials in his life, he admits that there, in the hospital yet again, because of an aggressive flare-up of the cancer, he feels only death.

While stories of faith and adversity often cling to the nomos located in the claim that "the hard times make you strong," Wiman confesses that he's unsure about *what*, if anything, all this suffering is teaching him. In the epigraph that began this section, Wiman's meditation on the meaning of suffering is framed more by questions than answers. Shall he trust that the meaning of suffering is somehow linked to this condition he's calling "faith"? Shall this odyssey of cancer-induced suffering lead him to more certainty that God and his own suffering are devoid of all meaning other than the ones he ascribes to them?

Glimpses of "I'll Go On": My Bright Abyss

Wiman confesses that he's a Christian not because of the resurrection (he wrestles with that), and not because Christianity is truer than other religions (he's open to truth coming in many forms). He's a Christian, he writes, "because of that moment on the cross when Jesus, drinking the very dregs of human bitterness, cries out, *My God, my God, why have you forsaken me?*" This moment of Christ's passion has meaning in his own life, Wiman suggests, because it tells him that "the absolute solitary and singular nature of extreme human pain is an illusion."[57] Christ's suffering and death on the cross reveal that love—divine in origin and incarnated in human flesh—is able to reach right into the depths of death.

This conviction is at the heart of the faith that grants Wiman the ability to resist cancer's attempt to claim meaninglessness as the final word in life. Even though he's intimately aware of the isolating nature of the pain he endures because of cancer, Wiman cautions against making idols of our own experience, of assuming our pain is more singular than it is. He is far from the only one living with cancer, far from the only one whose life has been undone at too young an age, with too much life yet to live.

It's the recognition of God's lack of immunity to human suffering that helps Wiman glimpse a way to go on. What makes Christianity meaningful for him is its insistence on the humanity of God—the insistence that God doesn't "float over the chaos of pain" and that God is, instead, "given over to matter."[58] This God is enmeshed in our reality rather than outside or beyond it. But this is no sentimental claim, as Jesus' cry on the cross demonstrates. God's absence, Wiman proposes, remains the primary form that God takes in the world.

Yet for Wiman this godless void and the experience of divine love come together in human acts that channel a greater mercy. Shortly after his diagnosis, Wiman meets the pastor of his newly chosen church. The pastor struggles with words true to his calling that would speak to the awfulness now attached to Wiman's life. Wiman describes what happened as they parted: "[The pastor] placed his hand over his heart for just a second and a flicker of empathetic anguish crossed his face. It sliced right through me. It cut through the cloud I was living in and let the plain day pour its balm upon me."[59]

The phrase "my bright abyss" is Wiman's attempt at naming toward God. In the final paragraphs of his book by that name, he recounts the scene where he and his wife lay in bed the first night home from the hospital after his transplant, both feeling a "bright defiance." A defiance neither of death nor of suffering but of *meaningless* death and suffering. Defiance, he writes, that warrants the name "faith," faith in the "bright abyss," where he comes to the edge of all he knows, "and believing nothing believe(s) in this."[60]

Millions of us live with cancer, but the majority of cancer stories never make it onto blogs or into books or TED Talks. Even as the stories told above represent only a fraction of the cancer stories in our midst, they allow us to appreciate more deeply some of the pressure points within cancer stories where experiences of meaninglessness and disorientation are most keenly felt. At the same time, these stories point to ways in which those who are seriously ill do not simply endure the anomie that threatens to overwhelm. They also offer glimpses of how those who are ill "go on," forging moments of meaning in the face of cancer's constant challenge to the nomos that was present in life before cancer.

The stories in this chapter also reveal that illnesses often operate largely outside a moral framework. "Let's face it. We're undone by each other," writes Judith Butler, referring to victims of violence whom those of us in the United States and the so-called "first world" too often ignore.[61] We need voices like Butler's and work by trauma researchers who expose the long-lasting effects of such violence. But the stories in this chapter about living with cancer remind us that not all undoing is caused by immoral human acts. Some undoings work from the inside out; the threat emerges internally and undoes not just the body but the psyche and the spirit. And such internal undoings need a kind of attention that we as a society and as religious communities are still working on.

A couple of years into my own undoing by cancer I was introduced to research on illness-related trauma. Diving into studies about how trauma works in the lives of those undone by cancer was like reading a version of my life with cancer that, for the first time, actually made sense. Trauma theorist Cathy Caruth describes what those who work with trauma try to do with and for those living with the aftereffects of traumatic emotional wounds: "[We try] to understand the nature of the suffering without eliminating the force and truth of the reality that trauma survivors face and quite often try to transmit to us."[62] She and others who work with the traumatized do this in order to facilitate healing.

The cancer stories explored above open up more breathing room for "I can't go on" moments and make it more possible to consider how living with cancer often means living with experiences of illness-related trauma. It is a task that is vital for theologians, ministers, churches, and all who care for those struggling with life-threatening illness. The next chapter returns to these four plotlines and demonstrates how recent work on illness-related trauma can aid us in going even deeper into these challenges as well as provide insight on how those who experience trauma might live with (and possibly even beyond) it.

CHAPTER 2

∞∞∞

LIVING WITH TRAUMA
BROUGHT ON BY ILLNESS

In the aftermath of trauma, death and life no longer stand in opposition. Instead, death haunts life. The challenge for those who experience trauma is to move in a world in which the boundaries and parameters of life and death no longer seem to hold, to provide meaning. The challenge for those who take seriously the problem of trauma is to witness trauma in all its complexities—to account for the ongoing experience of death in life.

—Shelly Rambo[1]

The emotional wounds of trauma involve threats of death, serious injury, or physical integrity and evoke reactions of intense fear, helplessness, and horror. As the cancer stories from the previous chapter illustrate, living with serious illnesses like cancer often precipitates an intense blurring of distinctions between death and life that is the hallmark of trauma. Therefore, it's not surprising that recent medical studies have explored how living with serious illnesses like cancer can produce symptoms of post-traumatic stress.

The vocabulary of trauma, however, has not yet made its way into most of the stories we tell about being ill. Why is that? One reason for this lack of talk about trauma's relationship to illness has to do with how the trauma story is most often told. While Shelly Rambo's description above makes space for a wide range of trauma-inducing experiences, much of the trauma literature focuses on trauma brought on by various forms of moral evil, devoting less attention to story lines featuring trauma related to the internal threat of illness.

Certainly the trauma that emerges from the sickening abundance of moral evil deserves our time and attention. As far back as the eighth century BCE, Homer was writing about the terrors of war and how those experiences haunted the ones who witnessed them. But it has only been little over a century that psychological conceptions of the traumatic aftereffects of (particularly *violent*) awful events have become an integral part of public consciousness. And as trauma theorist Judith Herman argues, contemporary understandings of psychological trauma have been shaped by significant historical moments when trauma caused by moral evils like war and sexual violence have taken center stage.[2]

In the initial diagnostic formulation of post-traumatic stress disorder (PTSD), all of the stressors were characterized as catastrophic (i.e., beyond the range of usual human experiences) and as originating from a source external to the individual. Authors of the original PTSD diagnosis had in mind events like war, rape, torture, the Nazi Holocaust, and natural and human-made disasters. These events were understood to be traumatic in ways very different from stressors that emerge from "the normal vicissitudes of life"—divorce, rejection, illness, financial challenges, and more. A central operative assumption was that although most people are able to cope with ordinary stress, one's ability to cope is much more likely to be overwhelmed when confronted by extraordinary external stressors.[3]

These descriptions of PTSD were not without controversy. Questions arose over the way in which characterization of symptoms seemed to be drawn heavily from experiences of combat. When the *DSM-IV* (*Diagnostic and Statistical Manual of Mental*

Disorders, 4th ed.) was published in 1994, the definition of *stressor* was expanded, no longer limited to firsthand experiences of a traumatic event but including "a threat to the physical integrity of self or others."[4] The requirement that the stressor be outside the range of usual human experience was also eliminated, allowing life-threatening illness to be considered a threat to life and bodily integrity.

Inclusion of serious illness in the list of stressors in the *DSM-IV* led to a number of studies on the relationship between illness and symptoms and diagnoses of post-traumatic stress. These studies indicate that many who live with serious illness experience one or more symptoms of post-traumatic stress, which now fall into four clusters: reexperiencing, avoidance, negative cognitions and mood, and arousal. The cluster of reexperiencing includes flashbacks or other intense spontaneous memories as well as prolonged psychological distress. The cluster of avoidance attends to experiences of distressing thoughts, feelings, or external reminders of the event. The negative-cognitions cluster covers a range of feelings from blame of self or others to estrangement from others or diminished interest in activities. Finally, the cluster of arousal includes hypervigilance, difficulty sleeping, and aggressive, self-destructive behavior.[5]

While many of us living with cancer experience one or more of these symptoms, research has demonstrated that the majority who live with serious illnesses do not exhibit enough symptoms to be diagnosed with a post-traumatic stress *disorder*. In the *DSM-5*, published in 2013, further modifications were made to the PTSD diagnosis, including the characterization of life-threatening illness as not necessarily a traumatic event.[6]

Even as research has shown that most of us living with life-threatening illnesses do not have a diagnosable post-traumatic stress disorder, it's worth lingering over whether or not serious illnesses should qualify as traumatic events. One of the main reasons for resisting a strong link between trauma and illness has to do with viewing illness as a natural part of human experience over against external, overwhelming traumatic events threatening from outside the self. Studies on illness-related trauma, however, demonstrate that those who live with cancer exhibit symptoms of traumatic stress.[7] A number of medical studies position life-threatening illness as a traumatic event that involves threats of death, serious injury, or physical integrity.[8]

Why do I think the potential relationship between illness and trauma deserves our attention? One reason has to do with the compelling medical research that illustrates the connection. Another reason is more personal: over the past nine years I have been very fortunate to receive great medical treatment for the metastasizing cancer threatening to overtake my body. I have been able to move into remission, not just once, or twice, but three times. I'm getting lots of opportunities to figure out what it means to live with incurable cancer. But the aftereffects of being diagnosed with and treated for cancer and the suffering that remains are often *more* challenging and longer lasting than the physical toll cancer takes on my body. As I become more familiar with research on illness-related trauma, and as I talk with more people living with cancer, I am repeatedly reminded that it's the invisibility of these wounds that exacerbates feelings of isolation, despair, and anomie.

I propose that paying closer attention to the invisible wounds that haunt those who live with cancer will not only increase self-understandings of the toll illness takes on those who are seriously ill and those who love and care for them, but it also can open up possibilities for new expressions of care for those living with cancer and other serious illnesses. Therefore, to flesh out what researchers have discovered about how trauma associated with serious illnesses like cancer operates and where it intersects with and diverges from other types of trauma, we will look again at the four previous "I can't go on" story lines and explore what trauma research illumines about how and why ill people get to the point of not going on. What insights emerge from the four "I can't go on" moments—bodily deterioration, refusal to ascribe to the positive cancer story, inability to imagine the future, and wrestling with the meaning of the cancer story—when the vocabulary of trauma becomes integral to how these stories are told?

"I Can't Go On" Story Line 1:
The Body Keeps the Score of Cancer-Related Trauma

In 2015, founder and medical director of the Trauma Center in Brookline, Massachusetts, Dr. Bessel van der Kolk, published *The Body Keeps the Score: Brain, Mind, and Body in the Healing of Trauma*, an influential medical memoir that testifies to how understanding post-traumatic stress has revolutionized care for those suffering the aftereffects of traumatic events. Van der Kolk recounts decades of work with military veterans, survivors of sexual and domestic violence, and individuals and families in close proximity to the Twin Towers on September 11, 2001, all of whom live with manifestations of post-traumatic stress. He chronicles how ongoing research about the manifestations of trauma on those who live with it has made a significant difference in their treatment and even, sometimes, in their ability to recover.

One of the main contributions of the book is van der Kolk's engagement with recent work in neuroscience that demonstrates how living in the aftermath of traumatic events involves living with a brain that operates differently due to having gone through such an event. He insists that while medical and psychiatric professionals have until recently largely ignored the relevance of the living, breathing body in attempts to treat post-traumatic stress, neuroscientific evidence reveals how the trauma that starts "out there" in combat or bodily violation migrates to being played out "on the battlefield" of the bodies of the traumatized.[9]

I appreciate van der Kolk's insistence that we pay attention to how the body keeps the score of traumatic experiences. As the stories from the previous chapter attest, what happens to the *bodies* of those who have cancer lies at the heart of what it means to be sick. But when the trauma conversation focuses on describing how trauma operates in tandem with life-threatening illnesses, it's necessary to pay attention to the distinctive ways in which the bodies of those with cancer keep the score.

It certainly is the case that aspects of cancer-related trauma are understood as coming from "out there." Receiving a devastating diagnosis can become a traumatic memory that is repeatedly reexperienced, disrupting the body's ability to function in predictable ways. Undergoing treatment for cancer can alter how the brain reacts to sensory perception, just as van der Kolk describes in his research. Research on cancer-related trauma has shown that minor routine procedures like maintenance scans and blood draws often lead to arousal symptoms of post-traumatic stress.[10] Learning that such reactions are common ones for cancer patients helped me better understand my own intensely physical reactions to "just getting poked" for an IV. For several years I was disturbed at my strong reaction: how could it be that I was able to birth my first child without an ounce of medication but now am unable to keep my heart from racing, breath from constricting, and eyes from filling with tears when I have to get a second or third poke for an IV? Illness-related trauma research helps me understand how my body is keeping the score of living with stage-IV cancer.

At the same time, van der Kolk's repeated casting of the cause of the trauma as "out there," as external to the body, illustrates the gap that often exists when comparing trauma caused by acts of violence to trauma caused by a life-threatening illness. Studies of cancer-related trauma show that for those living with cancer, the threat is perceived as primarily an *internal* one, a threat that permits "little chance of escapability."[11] While memory of the diagnosis may initially be a traumatic stressor that is reexperienced or avoided, over time this stressor often morphs into a hypervigilant fear of recurrence alongside fear of the deterioration of health that leads to death.

Knowing that the *enemy* or the *evil* (whether cancer should be understood in these moral terms is addressed again later in the chapter) is within us rather than outside us changes the dynamic of how the body keeps score of the trauma. Being ruled by her ill body, Susan Gubar admits, is a kind of "life-in-death." She confesses to the unspeakability of her bodily suffering after debulking surgery. So how are those who live with cancerous cells that threaten their existence supposed to address the trauma that comes from an ill and compromised body?

Understanding the threat as primarily an internal one affects what kind of help might be offered to those who live with serious illnesses like cancer. For van der Kolk, to deal with the trauma brought on by awful events is to address the following question: "How can traumatized people learn to integrate ordinary sense experiences so they can live with the natural flow of feeling and *feel secure and complete in their bodies*?" (emphasis mine).[12] When the threat is understood as most fundamentally an internal one, it becomes less certain that these persons will ever be able to feel "secure" or "complete" in their bodies again.

As the cancer stories told in chapter 1 illustrate, bodies are powerful reminders for those living with cancer of the trauma initiated by the diagnosis. Van der Kolk and other medical professionals are committed to figuring out how to alter—or even eliminate—the imprint left by the traumatic experiences on the mind, the brain, and the body. But when it comes to the "imprints" on the body of trauma from cancer, these invisible emotional imprints are often intimately connected to visible, physical ones. The stories of Susan Gubar and Audre Lorde highlight that the removal of body parts as well as various compromises to the body's ability to function in basic and predictable ways are aspects of just *how* the body keeps score of the trauma related to serious illness.

Lorde's description of wrestling with the persistent sorrow accompanying the loss of her breast witnesses to the ways her body keeps the score. On one level, she struggles with how to approach the world with a very visible imprint of her cancer: her new bodily reality of being one-breasted. At the same time, Lorde confirms van der Kolk's description of how trauma changes a person's capacity to think. She repeatedly worries about whether or not she lost her breast in vain (i.e., that it will not keep cancer at bay), and she admits to being sidelined by the question "How do I live one-breasted?" It's the invisible psychic wound of having one's identity altered by cancer that often fails to get adequate attention.

Shelly Rambo's perspective on trauma helps frame and interpret some of the challenges Lorde faces after her mastectomy:

"The experience of trauma can be likened to a death," Rambo writes. "But the reality is that the death is not ended; instead, it persists. The experience of survival is one in which life, as it once was, cannot be retrieved. However, the promise of life ahead cannot be envisioned."[13] This depiction of "death in life" adds a layer of gravity to Lorde's experience of trying to figure out what it means to live as a one-breasted woman in a world where all she's known is being two-breasted.

Lorde was diagnosed with breast cancer in 1978 before reconstructive surgery became integral to helping women who undergo mastectomies envision how to live after losing their breast(s). Lorde chose not to undergo reconstructive surgery, and even though she was fitted with a prosthetic breast, she was not inclined to wear it. That decision, however, proved problematic for some in the medical community. In her *Cancer Journals*, Lorde recounts the pressure placed on her by medical professionals to wear the prosthetic breast. During a postoperative visit to the oncology clinic, she is reprimanded for not wearing a prosthetic in the waiting room. "It's bad for morale in the office if you don't wear a prosthesis," she's told. The recurrent pressure on Lorde to treat her mastectomy as a cosmetic issue—nurses use the analogy that a prosthetic breast should be viewed as similar to an eye patch—affords women like her little "psychic time or space to examine [their] feelings" about their bodies keeping score of the cancer in this embodied, visible way. Other prosthetics are about function, Lorde points out. But "when I mourn my right breast, it's not the appearance I mourn."[14]

Because of the integral role that breasts play in women's identities—a reality that mattered greatly to Lorde herself—the last several decades have seen the medical community come to embrace the view that breast reconstruction should be an integral aspect of breast cancer treatment. In fact, women's advocates fought for and won the passage of the Women's Health and Cancer Rights Act of 1998 that requires health-insurance plans to cover prosthetics and reconstructive surgery procedures. Since the passage of this act, reconstruction has become standard care for women who have mastectomies.

That the majority of women who lose their breasts to cancer opt for reconstructed breasts[15] is not surprising. To have one or no breast is a very public indicator of how the body keeps the score of the aftereffects of cancer. Interestingly, however, there's a movement among twenty-first-century women who've had mastectomies to "go flat," that is, to live in the world flat-chested, with the evidence of the changes cancer wrought in their bodies publicly on display. Why are more women choosing this option? Some fear possible complications of reconstructive surgery; others claim that "breasts aren't what make us a woman."[16] It is a choice that potentially makes more space for acknowledgments of the trauma they've experienced related to how cancer is keeping the score in their own bodies. Just as was the case with Audre Lorde, women opting to "go flat" are not necessarily against reconstruction. Lorde objected to the insistence that women *must* render invisible the way their bodies keep the score of illness and its attendant trauma.

In his life as a pastor before a "stage serious" cancer diagnosis of his own in his late thirties, Jason Micheli had become aware of some of the ways in which cancer—especially breast cancer—takes a toll on a woman's relationship to her body-self. But he was unprepared for how his own cancer and treatment experiences has messed with his sense of being a man. In his recent memoir, Micheli dares to do what few men who write about cancer have done: offer candid confessions about how cancer forces a reconsideration of his identity, particularly his *gendered* identity. In one instance, he describes a night in bed with his wife where unsuccessful attempts at being physically intimate left him in tears, "which only left [him] feeling less of a man." The treatment regimen he was on also led to such muscle atrophy that he "had a hard time with that most mythic of masculine activities, tossing a baseball to [his] boys."[17]

The most striking illustration of how the physical toll of cancer upends his sense of himself as a man comes in a scene toward the end of the chemo regimen that leaves Micheli "smooth and hairless," considerably thinner, and sporting a "chemo glow" that makes it look like he's "wearing rouge." He attends an outdoor concert, with a knitted cap covering his bald head, and the bartender from whom he orders a drink asks him, "Will that be cash or credit, ma'am?" Certain that he misheard what the bartender had just said, he asks her to repeat herself. The bartender repeats the question, referring to him again as "ma'am."

"I blinked," he writes. "The bartender froze, as did the sangria smoothie machine behind her. Time stopped. The rain fell languidly. The encore from the opening band gave way to the sounds of my already-cracked self-image shattering."[18] Even as Micheli thoughtfully interrogates his own investment in conventional standards of what it means to be a man, his reflections on the psychic costs of having cancer offer valuable insight into how male bodies also keep score of cancer-related trauma.

Micheli's shattered sense of self is strongly linked to the effects of his treatment for the cancer. As he struggles toward the kind of reassessment of his body that van der Kolk recommends, Micheli seeks and finds solace for his shattered self in the Christian story of incarnation and claims that a flesh-and-blood body, just like his, is good enough to be a vessel of the Holy. While his oncologist predicted that after treatment he would return to who he was before the cancer, Micheli is keenly aware that he's been changed by the experience—physically, psychically, and spiritually—and he works toward a revised sense of himself as a man. "For instance," he writes, "without feeling embarrassed or emasculated, I can now cry."[19]

While it's not clear how long the side effects linger for Micheli, it is important to acknowledge that many types of cancers (particularly bladder, colon, rectal, and prostate) often cause sexual side effects for men, not just during treatment but sometimes for months, years, or even the remainder of one's life. Researchers at the Mayo clinic also note that sexual side effects are caused not just by physical changes in the body due to cancer and treatment but also by emotional factors.[20] Using the vocabulary of trauma helps deepen our understanding of just how the body keeps the score of the intimate connections between the physical and psychic wounds of cancer.

"I Can't Go On" Story Line 2:
Realistic—and Traumatic—Cancer Stories

Talk of how the body keeps the score of cancer helps move us closer to telling more realistic cancer stories, the kind Barbara Ehrenreich recommends. The following plot development in my own cancer story suggests that using the vocabulary of trauma helps guide the development of cancer stories in a more realistic direction:

> The cancer counselor is commenting on my indecision over whether or not to have my breasts removed. I have breast cancer, but few of my medical appointments have anything to do with breasts. This ignore-the-breasts approach strikes advocates of my life as problematic—reckless, even. Getting rid of the tumorous breast, or better yet, both breasts, is an integral part of the breast-cancer drill. It's what proactive breast cancer patients do. Meanwhile doctors remain single-mindedly focused on the breast cancer *in my bones* and resist weighing in on whether or not a mastectomy should be part of my treatment.
>
> I don't want a mastectomy. But those who love me won't let it go. This is one of the many reasons I'm in the cancer counselor's office talking about breasts. About the only thing I've decided since the diagnosis is that I don't want stage-IV cancer. But I'm stonewalled every time I try to return it. So instead of feeling proactive and making decisions about my life, I cry my way through my oncology appointment and leave with a referral to a cancer counselor so I can process the nonreturnable status of my diagnosis.
>
> The cancer counselor points out that removing breasts is often a traumatic experience. She suggests that the past several months of a broken back, radiation, back surgery, hospitalization, an endoscopy, and chemo have likely supplied me with plenty of trauma to deal with. Maybe it's OK to give myself permission to hold off on breast surgery.

Trauma. The word lingers, acting like a three-way bulb turned to the lowest setting in the corner of my mind. My mind is typically an organized, well-lit space. But advanced-stage cancer has ransacked the place and removed all the bulbs from the lamps. It's been virtually impossible to locate my file folders, especially the ones labeled *How to Make Decisions* and *Words to Describe What's Going On.*

But the light from the *trauma* bulb brings a few items back into focus. I'm able to make out the *Metastatic-Breast-Cancer Drill Is a Different Drill* banner that stretches from one end of my mind to the other. It's been hanging there since the day I was diagnosed; I just keep losing track of it in the dark. Seeing the banner again helps me realize that if research shows that removing my breasts would increase my chances of seeing my daughters graduate from high school, doctors would have opinions about getting rid of them.

As my eyes adjust to the lighting, I come across a new folder labeled *Permission to Postpone.* I take it with me and head back out into the gray February day.

In my own case, the cancer counselor's offering of the term *trauma* opened up new pathways of understanding for me about how cancer's invasion into my life was affecting my ability to function. Telling cancer stories with the help of the vocabulary of trauma can provide a little more light, a bit more breathing room to understand the toll of cancer, the way it undoes not just the body but the mind. Using the vocabulary of trauma can also counteract some of the societal pressure to tell primarily positive stories about our illnesses.

Arthur Frank's research on the sociology of illness grows out of his own experience of being diagnosed with cancer at age thirty-nine. In his book *At the Will of the Body: Reflections on Illness*, he discusses two kinds of emotional work that are involved in being sick. The first is work related to the fear, frustration, and loss that illness ushers into our lives. Such work is no small task.[21] The second kind of emotional work Frank discusses is the kind Ehrenreich attempts to interrogate; it's the need to keep up appearances that life is continuing on with as little interruption as possible. Or even continuing in an upward trajectory toward a new and improved you. Frank notes that while a common sentiment expressed to those who are ill is, "You don't look sick at all!" (Translation: "You're keeping up appearances"), his insight on the first kind of emotional work demanded by illness is particularly instructive in thinking about trauma as "the suffering that remains."[22] "I've never heard an ill person praised for how well she expressed fear or grief or was openly sad," Frank writes.[23] He suggests that what is often missing from our conversations is open acknowledgment of the persistent emotional wound—the *trauma*—that accompanies journeys with illness.

Frank suggests that it is precisely those wounds that make this kind of emotional work so difficult. He's struck by how few of us seem to accept that depression might well be the ill person's most appropriate response to being ill. Frank confirms Ehrenreich's observation that rather than making space for expressions of depression, society puts pressure on the ill to tell a positive story, to keep up appearances that all is manageable, even in the throes of cancer treatment. "What makes me saddest," Frank confesses, "is seeing the work ill persons do to sustain this cheerful patient image."[24] Keeping up appearances takes energy which, Frank points out, is already a scarce commodity when you're ill. And trying to be cheerful about life-threatening illness can lead to denial of the suffering that remains. Keeping up our defenses can make it even harder to face the realities of our illness.

Focusing on how trauma works on those living with serious illness deepens our appreciation of how challenging it is to be very sick. It also heightens our sensibilities of how trauma related to illness can be compounded when mingled with other types of trauma. In a recent study on those living in poverty in urban areas who also live with advanced cancer, oncology nurses report that it is not only frequent lack of supportive family structures but also the prevalence of other traumas (violence against themselves or close family members, wartime military service, etc.) that compound the trauma of dealing with a life-threatening illness. Moreover, those who live in poverty in urban areas are diagnosed with more advanced cancer and have lower rates of survival than those living in more affluent communities. The nurses authoring the study insist that "understanding the everyday lives of patients is necessary to develop realistic and practical self-care plans and to identify needed community resources."[25] Paying closer attention to traumatic dimensions of living with serious illness helps us do just that.

One of the convictions guiding Ehrenreich's insistence on telling a more realistic cancer story is directly related to this sense of denial of the many ways that cancer wounds lives — physically, emotionally, psychologically, and spiritually. While many of us living with cancer may balk at Ehrenreich's proposal to call ourselves "victims" of cancer, opting instead for terms with more agency, Ehrenreich reaches for "victim" language partly because it emphasizes that we've been acted upon by the cancer, the treatment, and the trauma brought on by them both.

Ehrenreich also advocates for victim language over against the warrior imagery that suggests we actually have control over our condition. The vocabulary of fighting versions of cancer stories insists that we "join the fight" against cancer. When people die of cancer, their obituaries often testify that they "fought valiantly" against cancer but ultimately "succumbed" to its force. These images often fail to capture adequately the emotional challenges of what it's like to live in the midst of illnesses like cancer.

Shortly before being diagnosed with cancer, Frank — a runner who appeared to be in great health — suffered a heart attack. Thus part of his insight into the social dynamics of cancer comes from his experience of dealing with multiple serious illnesses within a short period of time. In *At the Will of the Body*, Frank describes the sharp contrast between having heart disease and having cancer. When his heart disease became known, no one talked to him about "fighting" it. People with diseases other than cancer are often "just plain sick," Frank observes, while those with cancer are supposed to "fight it."[26] Why the difference? Frank and others propose that the difference is the stigma—the mark of shame—attached to cancer that isn't attached to other diseases.[27]

Frank argues that society views cancer as a contaminant while conditions like heart disease are simply seen as bad luck. He builds on the work of writer and filmmaker Susan Sontag and her exploration of the metaphorical force of the word *cancer*, which she refers to as "the most radical of disease metaphors."[28] Cancer has long been employed metaphorically to describe seemingly intractable societal ills, from the political climate in the Middle East to the insidiousness of racism in the United States. While Sontag's incisive critique of the "militaristic hyperbole" used in relation to the cancer metaphor remains apt, her now forty-year-old vision for how language about cancer will evolve is particularly prescient.

Sontag insists that the vision of cancer as an insidious, intractable evil must change, especially as the disease becomes better understood and rates of cure increase. She predicts that as treatment shifts from the chemotherapeutic approach of "killing" cancerous and healthy cells alike to "some kind of immunotherapy" that relies on the body's "natural defenses," cancer will become more "de-mythicized." It may even become possible, she writes, "to compare something to a cancer without implying either a fatalistic diagnosis or a rousing call to fight by any means whatever a lethal, insidious enemy."[29] Emerging research on illness-related trauma is contributing to the formation of a different, nonmilitary-focused vocabulary to talk about what it means to negotiate life with a serious illness.

In addition to the weakening-but-still-present metaphorical stigma of the term *cancer*, Frank also discusses the way in which those of us with the disease tend to "wear cancer" in more visible ways (hair loss during treatment being a prime example) than those with more "invisible" illnesses like heart disease. How cancer alters one's body is no small matter. At the same time, it is important to acknowledge that cancer is not the only disease weighed down by stigma and that, at present, other "invisible" diseases like mental illness require those who live with them to navigate powerful stigmas around the social acceptability of the disease.

Even though he critiques societal pressures to tell positive, fighting cancer stories, Frank wants to hold on to the claim that we have some choice in how we experience illness.[30] As Matthew, a husband who cares for his wife who lives with cancer, observes, "It is not winning or losing the battle against cancer, it's learning to live with it."[31] Becoming more aware of the traumatic dimensions of the chronicity of living with diseases like cancer can lead those who are ill to seek out resources to address the symptoms of post-traumatic stress that affect them. And the vocabulary of cancer-related trauma can help us more fully incorporate into our cancer stories the subplot of psychic distress that living with cancer engenders. Being able to express experiences of sadness, depression, and grief opens avenues not only for medical professionals to recommend mental-health support (as my oncologist did) but also for caregivers and loved ones to have a more realistic view of what it means for those who are sick to live with their illness.

One way psychic distress is often treated today is with medication. Studies of the treatment of cancer-related trauma have yet to include research on cancer patients' use of psychopharmaceuticals to treat symptoms of post-traumatic stress; however, cancer researchers cite studies for treatments of post-traumatic stress generally that suggest the ineffectiveness of antidepressant medication like SSRIs for the majority of patients dealing with post-traumatic stress. What researchers propose instead are therapeutic approaches that focus on meaning making amid the experience of trauma.[32]

A realistic cancer story is a story that dares to tell of the trauma related to diagnosis, treatment, and ongoing management of the disease. At the same time, it is a story that also identifies ways to cope with this life-altering reality of being seriously ill. Studies of cancer patients have shown that many people who live with cancer report having experienced "post-traumatic growth" in the aftermath of their diagnosis. In other words, people living with cancer report that they are finding ways to adapt and find meaning and value in their lives in the aftermath of illness-related trauma.[33] That many experience such growth lends credence to the claim that our lives are bigger than the trauma. Paying attention to illness-related trauma clarifies that experiences of positive growth, while significant in their own right, do not diminish or efface the pain and suffering that being seriously ill injects into one's life. Before attending more thoroughly to the kinds of post-traumatic growth those living with cancer experience, it's important to explore other consequences of illness-related trauma, such as its effect on one's ability to imagine the future.

"I Can't Go On" Story Line 3:
Trauma, Cancer, and the Future

In writing about life after his diagnosis of metastatic lung cancer, Paul Kalanithi expresses relief when no one at his college reunion asks him about his plans for the future because, he admits, he has none.[34] When people receive a life-altering diagnosis of incurable cancer, it's not surprising that they often experience a common consequence of post-traumatic stress: an inability to imagine the future.[35]

While some forms of cancers quickly overtake one's neurological capabilities, and other cancer diagnoses lead almost immediately to the grave, it is also the case that advances in medical technology are offering those of us with life-threatening illnesses increased opportunities for prolonged life. That more of us are living longer with advanced-stage cancer means more of us are living with what health and illness sociologist Rebecca Olson is calling "indefinite loss."[36] Olson's conceptualization of this type of loss shares much in common with Shelly Rambo's description of trauma.[37] That indefinite loss is the condition "where cancer and death are no longer synonymous but the possibility of death is ever-present"[38] suggests that it is a condition where death haunts life. As cancer treatments and rates of living longer with the disease continue to advance, a cancer diagnosis shifts from being associated with an almost-certain, imminent death to life with a potentially limited future. What does it mean to occupy this liminal (and often traumatic) space?

All of the cancer stories explored thus far attest to the difficulty of going on in the face of a diminished body, a diminished present, and a diminished future brought on by cancer and its accompanying treatments. These stories demonstrate that many present-day journeys with cancer follow unpredictable paths where the future depends on multiple probabilities and uncertainties. Periods of wellness do not necessarily indicate longevity, just as periods of being really sick during treatment do not necessarily indicate a foreshortened future. As Olson proposes, neither statistics nor observable indicators necessarily offer reliable assurance about the future. And this liminal space provides ample opportunity to experience the trauma related to indefinite loss.[39]

Recall that for Todd Billings the period following a successful stem-cell transplant was the most trying he had experienced since his diagnosis of multiple myeloma.[40] While many of us would likely predict that a successful transplant outcome would offer new reasons for hope, Billings confesses that as a future of more living opens up, he is tempted to despair. His fear of what's ahead becomes palpable. Has life been prolonged only to enable him to endure more procedures, more subsequent diminishments? Billings's emotional turmoil is tied up with the many losses he's facing. As Frank points out, cancer and its treatments can sever our sense of continuity with our own body's past. Cancer, surgery, chemo, and transplants all change more than the body; they change how we live.[41] And the vision of living a diminished life in a diminished body sidelines Billings. To go on into the "new normal" where *nothing* seems normal at all leads him to the agonizing question "For what?"[42]

One of the enduring effects of trauma, van der Kolk claims, is the way in which this emotional wound curtails our ability to imagine the future. "Imagination is absolutely critical to our lives," he writes. "It enables us to leave our everyday existence and imagine new possibilities. . . . Without imagination, there's no hope, no chance to envision a better future."[43] Imagination is especially needed when one's taken-for-granted future crumbles before one's eyes.

While Billings has faith that he is part of God's future, he struggles with what he *can* imagine about more life with incurable cancer. Billings's story illustrates how cancer takes us to the "threshold of life," where we're "alive but detached from everyday living," as Frank describes it.[44] The treatment Billings undergoes leaves him in severe pain, unable to work or to participate in many of the daily tasks of being part of a family, and mostly isolated from the people who constitute his life. In that space, figuring out how to go on can seem virtually impossible. Van der Kolk insists that for those whose traumatic experiences are external in nature, the goal is to renegotiate one's relationship to the external event from the past that caused the harm. This renegotiation makes space once again for imagining a future, but with the chronicity as well as the internality of experiences of illnesses like cancer, renegotiating the relationship with the source(s) of illness-related trauma presents a different kind of challenge.

Frank suggests that the fear experienced by those living with cancer is rarely about dying a sudden death. What's palpable, rather, is the fear of dying slowly, of watching as indefinite losses turn definite. He writes,

> I have now been with enough people dying of cancer to know that their deaths involve fewer of the gruesome details than I feared. Popular fears of cancer, which I shared, exaggerate the drama of its terrors but underestimate the mundane discomforts that accumulate. If a heart attack blows you away, cancer chips at you bit by bit.[45]

In the telling of her own story of life with incurable cancer, Carrie Host recounts the initial joy she experienced after receiving news of her cancer's remission. But it wasn't long before this really good news led "to a giant question mark preceded by two words, 'Now what?'" Host realizes that bad news isn't the only kind of news that forces someone living with cancer into facing "the unknown." Good news does that, too. Especially when the prognosis is grim, as it was in Host's case, "later" becomes "a mental luxury that you will no longer partake in."[46] It's not just a failure of imagination; it is also an attempt to take seriously the medical knowledge that tells you you're in grave shape.

By the time he learns that he has more living ahead of him, Billings is already keenly aware of the multitudinous ways cancer chips away at body, spirit, and soul. It is precisely this awareness of the progressive chipping away that inspires Billings's wrenching wonderment at how he'll go on. He talks about how his preoccupation with such thoughts only isolates him further from the others in his life who continue full speed ahead into the future. Similarly Carrie Host writes about how she felt after getting well enough to participate actively in her life again, which is full of those she loves: "I continuously feel sad when I should feel grateful."[47] What does it mean for those of us living with cancer to renegotiate our relationship with the cancer in such a way that we can imagine a way to live into the future, even if that future is significantly curtailed? Living with advanced-stage cancer means that the death that has inserted itself into life often cannot be removed. What then?

When van der Kolk turns to specific recommendations about how to facilitate healing in the lives and bodies of those who live with trauma, he insists that getting those who live with trauma to talk about the event(s) that caused the trauma is often helpful. Research on illness-related trauma shows that individual and group therapy that encourages those who are seriously ill to reframe their experiences and find meaning in their current life increases their ability to imagine a life that is bigger than the trauma and the cancer.[48]

In addition, many who have endured long journeys with cancer have also indicated that they wish they would have been able to talk with others who were farther down the cancer road during some of the worst parts of their own journey.[49] One of my first social occasions out of the house after my diagnosis was to have coffee with a woman from my church who was in her fifth year of living with advanced-stage cancer. Her presence was a living, breathing example of someone who, according to statistics, should be dead. But there she was, sitting across the table from me, embodying a future beyond the awful days of diagnosis and treatment. She recounted many details about life in and beyond treatment, but the statement that lodged itself in my brain was this: "There will come a day when cancer is not part of your every thought." On that bleak February day, less than two months into my own cancer story, I couldn't bring myself to believe her. I had resigned from my full and wonderful life; treatment for my incurable cancer was making me weaker, sicker by the day; my world had become consumed with all things cancer; and any imagining of the future was limited to all those future moments in my family's lives that I was convinced I'd miss.

When remission rather than death became my future, it was time to sign back up for the life from which I'd resigned—to go back to teaching, to go back to being an involved parent in my daughters' lives, to accept speaking engagements, to imagine and plan another family vacation. The unbelievable reality my friend told me about in that coffee shop gradually made its way into my life. She was right: cancer no longer dominated my every thought. Like Billings and Host, however, I found that signing back up for life was more difficult than I had anticipated. Before cancer, I had little firsthand experience with anxiety. The decision to return full time to the university, however, made me incredibly anxious (*What if the cancer flares up again in the middle of another semester? What if I have to resign from this life a second time—will I be able to endure it?*). Accepting a speaking engagement for the following calendar year ushered in new worries (*Will I still be in remission? Will I have enough energy to honor this commitment?*). The indefinite character of the loss makes reentry into everyday living difficult to negotiate. Rambo's definition of trauma as "the suffering that remains"[50] describes well the sense of irresolution brought on by chronic illness.

These days it's my turn to meet with friends, acquaintances, or even strangers and bear witness to life beyond the crucible of cancer treatment. Our conversations include shared stories of diagnosis, treatment, and prognosis. I repeat the words my friend told me that cold winter day: it's increasingly possible that a day will come when their every thought will not be dominated by cancer. But more recently I've come to add something about the sometimes unexpected difficulty of going on, of the suffering that remains, of the challenging and beautiful experience of a once-closed future opening up again.[51]

I also share what I've learned from van der Kolk and other trauma researchers: that to deal with this emotional work, those who live with trauma need to do more than talk. Even as medical and psychological treatments for post-traumatic stress have tended to focus on verbal therapies (which van der Kolk himself supports), especially when pursued on their own, they are often not enough. The final sections of van der Kolk's *The Body Keeps the Score,* therefore, are devoted to discussing the potential for other ways to address the trauma, particularly long-neglected practices like community rituals, music, movement, and other art forms that are capable of circumventing the traditional reliance on words.[52] That Billings finds comfort in religious practices like reciting psalms of lament and praying and in the conviction that he is not responsible for writing the final chapter of his life (God is)—these are all illustrations that help him imagine the future enough to go on.

"I Can't Go On" Story Line 4:
Trauma, Anomie, and Suffering with Cancer

One of the reasons trauma research is gaining attention in academic circles and beyond likely comes from the ways in which studying the aftereffects of events of moral evil helps sharpen the argument that such events *are* evil. To talk about the post-traumatic stress reactions to instances of sexual assault deepens our understanding that it is not simply a one-time violation of a person's bodily integrity. It's a violation that often creates a persistent wound that continues to be experienced psychologically, emotionally, spiritually, and physically.

Similarly, being forced to flee one's homeland because of war and being relocated to a refugee camp are not only physically taxing but often mean that people live with the immediacy of the death of their previous lives. Examining these events with assistance from trauma studies opens up more space to understand that suffering initiated by an evil of the past persists into the future in enduring ways and to advocate for more justice work that attempts to limit or even prevent such evils from happening in the first place. But the suffering that remains from enduring serious illness, where the cause often does not fit neatly within the framework of moral evil, presents distinctive challenges when attempting to make sense of the suffering.

Christian Wiman's story testifies to the menacing ways in which death haunts life when one is living with trauma brought on by the diagnosis of and treatment for advanced, incurable cancer.[53] Wiman lets readers in on his ongoing struggles to make sense of his life amid the cancer and the challenges of pain and anomie that push him to the brink of questioning whether his life of suffering has any meaning at all. That death is no longer relegated to the future leaves him undone, stuck in a state of uncertainty. Wiman is keenly aware of the fact that he's enduring a kind of suffering that does not fit neatly (or at all) into a framework of moral evil. He resists both secular and religious story lines about illness that strong-arm a framework of nomos onto the experience. Wiman's anguished questioning supports pastoral theologian Deborah van Deusen Hunsinger's claim in *Bearing the Unbearable: Trauma, Gospel, and Pastoral Care* that experiences of trauma often issue "a growing sense of disorientation or even meaninglessness" that lead to spiritual crises.[54]

Theologian Nicholas Wolterstorff, who lost his adult son in a tragic mountain-climbing accident, frames the challenge of suffering that falls outside the realm of moral evil this way:

> To the "why" of suffering we get no firm answer. Of course some suffering is easily seen to be the result of our sin: war, assault, poverty amidst plenty, the hurtful word. And maybe some is chastisement. But not all. The meaning of the remainder is not told us. It eludes us. Our net of meaning is too small. There's more to our suffering than our guilt.[55]

"There's more to our suffering than our guilt." Throughout much of Christian thought, suffering and death have been understood to be the result of the fall of human beings into sinfulness. More recently, however, death has come to be viewed as part of God's original intention for creation; we are part of the created order, and, as such, we're born, we live, and we die. Very often, then, we get sick not because we're sinners but because we're human.

So how is it that we are to make sense of our cancer-ridden lives? Once again it's important to highlight the reality that illnesses are very often *internal* threats from which there's little chance of escape. Research shows that "chronic illnesses of uncertain origin and outcome pose particularly difficult problems of meaning attribution."[56] As a poet and a person of faith, Wiman proposes that uncertainty goes hand-in-hand with faith. He also confesses that the Christian story—particularly the part where Christ experiences being abandoned by God while suffering on the cross—doesn't necessarily make sense out of life with cancer as much as help him understand that he is not alone in his suffering.

Pastors and others of us who understand the Christian story as normative for our lives can draw on Wiman's insights to bring this point more clearly to the fore for those who live with the trauma of life-threatening illness: The story that casts death as the final enemy (1 Cor. 15:26) is also the story where death is an intrinsic dimension of the life of God. It is in this death-dealing suffering that we can meet God. While this insight might not bring meaning to our suffering, it can bring comfort. Still, what can be so fear-inducing about such suffering is the way it threatens to separate us from the ones we love the most.

Illness-Related Trauma Affects More Than Just the One Who Is Ill

For the vast majority of those who live with cancer, the suffering caused by the illness is not theirs alone. Family members and close friends of the one who is ill also live with manifestations of trauma, of the suffering that remains. As reported in the *DSM-IV-TR*, reactions of individuals who indirectly experience a traumatic event are consistent with those who experienced the trauma directly.[57] In addition, whether and how those close to the one who is ill experience trauma depends at least partially on what researchers call their own "temperamental vulnerability" to psychic distress.

One of the biggest issues for close relatives, such as a spouse, who walk the cancer journey with the one who is ill, is the way in which having a loved one who is seriously ill challenges their own "taken-for-granted" notion of time. Those of us who are young or middle-aged, especially if we're middle- or upper-class, tend to be future-oriented.[58] As Christian Wiman confessed, before his own cancer diagnosis he lived in a land "where only other people die,"[59] leaving him free to plan for and envision an expansive future for himself and his family. But a cancer diagnosis disrupts this perception of the future, not only for the person with the diagnosis but for the spouse and other members of the family. An uncertain future for someone with cancer often leads that person's spouse to experience a similar lack of control and sense of loss over the future that was once envisioned. When Linda, whose husband has cancer, was asked in a workplace workshop to envision her goals one year, three years, and five years out, she admitted that she couldn't complete the exercise because she "had stopped looking ahead" and was trying to focus on the present and the time she had left with her ill spouse.[60]

Financial-planning decisions can also become difficult when a spouse has cancer. "Do I plan on my spouse's income or not?" is just one of many issues the spouse of the one who is sick is forced to contemplate. And having those doubts in the first place can lead to feelings of guilt. Researcher Rebecca Olson labels this experience of being unable to figure out one's relationship to the future because of a spouse's illness "temporal anomie," a challenged relationship to time based on a sense of normlessness and lost direction.[61] That more and more of us are living longer with cancer, even at advanced stages, means not only that those of us with cancer have more time to negotiate an uncertain future but that our spouses and family members are also faced with this challenge. Having more time is often a gift, but there are also situations when the person living with cancer is so compromised by the illness that it becomes very difficult for the spouse (who is often also the caregiver) to deal with.

In her exploration of the effects of this kind of indefinite loss, Olson interviews Phyllis, whose husband's personality changed in dramatic ways due to a neurological cancer. He became confused, and his cognitive abilities decreased. Phyllis admits, "You just think, 'I wish it would be over', but you feel really guilty, because you didn't want it to be really over but you wanted to be out of the situation and you didn't want them to be sick." Because she felt that she would be betraying her husband if she told others about these thoughts, she kept them to herself. Only after her husband's death did she begin to open up about what she was thinking and feeling during that time.[62]

An additional level of stress for both the parent who has cancer and the parent whose partner has cancer has to do with how the cancer diagnosis affects the children in the family. Cancer patients with children have significantly higher risk of developing a stress disorder during the course of living with the disease than those without children.[63] While the psychic and emotional tolls of a parent's cancer diagnosis on children are variable and not always easy to detect, research indicates that symptoms like sleep disturbances and emotional challenges in the form of depression and anxiety can linger long after a parent's cancer treatments have ended. This leads researcher Heide Goetz and her colleagues to suggest that "psycho-oncological" support during and after treatment is often vital not just for the one who has cancer but for all members of the family.[64]

One of the most compelling dimensions of Olson's research on indefinite loss is her protest against what she sees as a preoccupation in oncology literature with delivering cancer diagnoses in a way that "maintains hope" for both cancer patients and their family members. Olson is not opposed to hope, but before hope can be fostered, she argues, it's really the "temporal anomie" of patients and members of their families that needs to be explored. One needs to look at the ways that the ability of cancer patients and family members to imagine the future is stymied or how what spouses and children imagine accomplishes nothing other than stirring up feelings of guilt or anxiety. Only then will a conversation about hope (in what? for what?) be helpful.[65]

In addressing questions of recovery from trauma, researchers like Judith Herman argue that "resolution of the trauma is never final; recovery is never complete."[66] At the same time, emerging research points to the possibility of post-traumatic growth, a type of growth that does not return to one's pretrauma existence but nevertheless progresses toward a new identity and a new story. Numerous factors — such as the kind of support the person who is ill and their family members receive — influence what kind of growth might be possible. In addition to emotional support, those who are ill and their family members can benefit greatly from strategies that help process what it means to live with serious illness.[67] Research on those living with cancer indicates that, like Billings and Wiman, those who are able to go on in the face of cancer and other serious illnesses often rely heavily on religion and spirituality to help them make meaning in the wake of this internal threat. In many instances, religion helps contribute to a sense of purpose and provides a framework for understanding the experience of life-threatening illness, and even death.[68]

At the same time, research also reveals another dynamic that can be in play: religion can be used in harmful as well as helpful ways in the aftermath of a life-altering event. When religion is used to shun medical treatment out of confidence that God will certainly bring healing or when illness is viewed as punishment from a wrath-filled, unloving God, such religious views are shown to contribute to higher stress and even increased mortality rates in dealing with a serious diagnosis.[69] Considerable psychological research, however, suggests that positive religious coping strategies are ones that steer clear of such "negative" practices. But such studies also label emotions like doubt, anger, and hopelessness as well as protests against God as "negative" and potentially harmful. They show that being in a perpetually negative state of anger or hopelessness can be damaging to one's health.

Paying attention to the effects of illness-related trauma heightens our sensitivity to how and why such "negative" emotions are a part of one's experience of living with a life-threatening illness. It is also important to take into account that people's religious beliefs can and often do fluctuate, whether in dealing with illness or the ups and downs of life more generally. That people with life-threatening illnesses along with their family members and close friends experience anger at God today does not guarantee that anger becomes a primary approach of living with their illness.[70] When life is undone by cancer, these emotions are almost impossible to avoid.

Exploration of how trauma emerges in the lives of those living with cancer sets the stage for theological reflection on where and how the Christian story makes space for those living with negative emotions and illness-related trauma. Even as the Christian story is often characterized as a triumphant one that concludes resolutely with resurrection, closer examination of the biblical text reveals numerous places that acknowledge and support those who have become undone by illness or other awfulness. Consideration of psalms of lament, the story of Job, Jesus' cry of godforsakenness on the cross, and Christ's descent into hell all demonstrate what can—but should not—be an elusive truth: that the biblical story is spacious enough to hold the broken bodies and depleted emotional and spiritual conditions of the seriously ill and those who love them. As we will see, these moments in the biblical story also help reframe the experiences of being undone within the larger scope of the divine drama that says illness, trauma, and death are not the final word.

CHAPTER 3

⊂◯◯⊃

TRAUMA, ILLNESS, AND THE CHRISTIAN STORY

In a world where threats to nomos come at us from multiple sides, religion is often viewed as offering stability amid chaos and uncertainty by providing foundational stories that reaffirm we really do live in an ordered world rather than one overtaken by meaninglessness and anomie. Recall Kate Bowler's story of her Christian neighbor telling Bowler's husband that everything—even a young wife and mother's stage-IV cancer diagnosis—happens for a reason. The neighbor is simply unable to admit out loud how awful it is that Bowler has been knocked down by cancer because doing so tears at the fabric of meaning that religion is supposed to offer.

If religious communities are to be places where those who live with serious illness are able to transmit the force and truth of their reality and are held and supported in ways that might relieve the suffering, the religious stories we tell need to be spacious enough to hold the grief, loss, and temptations to despair that accompany traumatic experiences of being really sick. And one way to do this is to take on the central Christian theological plotline—the one about death being transformed into new life, the one that bends toward resolution — and let it breathe. For example, theologian Serene Jones, in her book *Trauma and Grace*, rehearses the version of the central Christian theological story line that most people of faith know by heart, a story of moral evil and its vanquishing.[1] It begins with God creating a good world, but the plot takes a troubling turn when humans usher sin into the world and mess everything up. The story's climax comes when God intervenes in the sinful world in the form of Jesus, who lives, dies, and is raised in order to save the world. It is a triumphant story, a story of resolution where grace ultimately conquers and overcomes sin.

The more deeply Jones has traveled into trauma literature (and endured a series of difficult personal experiences, including miscarriage and divorce), however, the more difficult it has become for her to find space within the sin-grace story as it is commonly told, even when it is critiqued for patterns of domination and reformed by contemporary insights from feminists and other theologians passionate about justice. She has become more aware that even in many contemporary retellings of the Christian story where concerns of justice are paramount, an optimistic, insistent commitment to the possibility of lasting change persists. The narrative focuses on how structures of injustice can be challenged, critiqued, and overcome on a trust that new life *will* emerge.

While Jones acknowledges the existential importance of the Christian story's movement from death to new life and its ability to empower those who have suffered greatly to move toward healing, she nevertheless worries that even these versions of the story "fail to account for the harsh fact that the vast majority of trauma survivors reach the end of their lives still caught in its terrifying grip."[2] As her understanding of the aftereffects of trauma has deepened and as moments in her personal life are defined by irresolution, Jones sobers in her confidence of trauma's "solvability" and wonders whether the sin-grace plotline of the Christian story creates adequate space for those undone by trauma. Jones's searching for spaces within the Christian story that resist solvability represents one approach taken by those who work with trauma and theology. Jones and other theologians like Shelly Rambo insist that respecting the seriousness, depth, and ways in which suffering remains with the traumatized requires more nuanced and spacious theological claims about how all of our suffering is wiped away.

Growing awareness of trauma and its aftereffects is happening alongside burgeoning interest by Christian theologians and practitioners to return to spaces of irresolution and lament within the biblical narrative. One of the most important recent examples of returning to lament is Kathleen Billman and Daniel Migliore's *Rachel's Cry: Prayer of Lament and Rebirth of Hope*. The book's title is drawn from the story in Jeremiah 31 of Rachel's cry over the loss of her children and her refusal to be consoled. Billman and Migliore point out that while the figure of Rachel and her disturbing cry is revered in Judaism, she and her bold, unsettling practice of lament is mostly overlooked in Christian theology and practice. Christian attention to this section of Jeremiah's story tends to focus instead on the promise of the new covenant rather than on Rachel's haunting, irresolute cry.[3] While reference to Rachel's weeping for her children in the book of Jeremiah emerges out of the context of Israel's exile, an event often cast within the moral framework of Israel's disobedience to God, Billman and Migliore are committed to making more visible biblical and theological resources for the practice of lament, the practice of directing one's anguish at God, whether the anguish emerges out of a context of violence or not.

After paying careful attention in chapter 1 to the moments where those living with cancer often feel that they can't go on and exploring in chapter 2 how insights from trauma research can illumine those experiences of being undone by illness, it is time to explore in this chapter places where traumatic experiences of illness might find space to breathe within the Christian story. Research shows that stories and practices of religion can enhance the psychological and spiritual resources of those who are seriously ill, helping them build a framework in which to interpret their experiences of trauma and illness, a framework that can facilitate hope.[4] But what I hear repeatedly from those who live with serious illness is that it's hard to get to hope if one's experience of being undone is neither acknowledged nor given space to breathe. Therefore, it is not only possible but *necessary* to reexamine our religious stories and pay particular attention to spaces that offer solace to those who live with the aftereffects of illness-related trauma.

In what follows, I explore spaces for lament in the Christian biblical story where those undone by serious illness can find haven. I return again to the four cancer story lines explored in the previous two chapters—the body's keeping score, the pressure to tell a positive cancer story, the foreclosure of the future, and the difficulty of finding meaning in the suffering—and link them to four particular moments in the biblical story: the psalms of lament, the story of Job, Jesus' cry of abandonment on the cross, and the space between crucifixion and resurrection. Each of these moments in the Christian story makes space for experiences of being physically undone and the traumatic suffering that accompanies them.

Placing these experiences of living with serious illness within particular biblical narratives also means that I am exploring what it means to be undone by illness *before God*. The central character in these biblical stories is God, the One who creates and calls human beings into relationship with the Divine and with one another. It's important to note, as preacher Thomas Long does, that questions of God's existence are not really on the table within the biblical text. The characters in the Bible do not ask, "I am undone by illness; I wonder if there's a God?" Instead they cry out, "O God, why illness?"[5] These moments within the biblical story are important not just because they open up space for those undone by serious illness to express their grief and anger; they are also important because they speak to God's relationship with and response to the people enduring illness and the trauma related to it.

This chapter, then, is about making space to protest *toward God*, to be angry *at God*, to complain *to God* over suffering that simply is but that we desperately wish would not be. While it is important to acknowledge that some who express such emotions do so because of a loss of or rejection of faith, it is also possible to express such emotions *within* the context of a relationship with God. As psychologist Julie Exline's research has shown, making more visible spaces within religion for such interrogation of God may well be crucial for those who tend to view any challenge of God as unfaithful. One concern Exline expresses in her research is whether or not individuals believe they have permission to protest or be angry at God. Granting such permission can be an important role for a pastor, chaplain, or other religious leader. Exline proposes that if people who are angry at God are given more opportunities to consider that their protest and anger can actually be part of a close, resilient relationship with God, they might be able to come to terms with protest as an aspect of a faithful relationship with God rather than evidence of a lack of faith.[6]

Space in the Psalms for the Body's Keeping Score

As mentioned above, most conventional renditions of the Christian story tend to follow a linear narrative arc, beginning with creation and the fall and quickly moving on to incarnation and redemption. Turning our attention first to the psalms reminds us that the biblical narrative is less plot driven and more complex than a tidy, linear, sin-redemption story line often allows. Billman and Migliore point out that prayer was a basic element of Israel's religious life and that individual and communal relationship with God was understood as one of ongoing conversation.[7] Because Old Testament writings are Christian Scripture too (four-fifths of Christian Scripture, in fact, a reality often overlooked by Christians), prayer practices of the Psalms belong in any version of the Christian story we are interested in telling.

Just as is the case for millions of Christians, prayer has always been part of my religious life. But a broken back and a stage-IV cancer diagnosis robbed me of words, not just words to talk about what was happening to my body and spirit but words to talk to God. Susan Gubar's attempts to describe the aftereffects of her debulking surgery likely speak for many of us who live with life-threatening illness. She's left with words like "unspeakable" and "unspeakably anxiety-producing" when trying to communicate how cancer undoes her body along with her own self-understanding.[8] Elaine Scarry, writing on the language of physical pain, observes that pain "does not simply resist language but actively destroys it."[9] Combine the intense physical pain of being ill with invisible wounds of illness-related trauma and words become scarce. That includes words directed toward God.

For months after my diagnosis, I found that the words of the psalms offered me a vocabulary to talk about what was happening to my body, spirit, and soul. The book of Psalms is called *Sepher Tehillim* in Hebrew, which means "Book of Praises," and it is known by people of faith as a book full of praise and thanksgiving for God, such as "O LORD . . . how majestic is your name" (Ps. 8:1) and "Blessed be the name of the LORD" (Ps. 113:2). The hundred and fifty prayers in the book of Psalms offer language not just for joy, gratitude, and praise but for the full range of life's emotions and experiences.

One of the most distinctive marks of Israel's practice of prayer is the inclusion of prayers of lament, protest, and even argumentation. "I am so troubled that I cannot speak," laments the psalmist in Psalm 77 (v. 4). Within the biblical practice of lament, Billman and Migliore note, it is always loss or diminishment of bodily life that is mourned.[10] That this book of praise includes so much lament about our embodied lives suggests that the Israelite notion of "praise" is much more spacious and complex than an understanding of "praise" as containing only positive sentiments. Thus theologians working with trauma have returned to the psalms and the space they make for lamenting the ways that human bodies and lives become undone by traumatic events. Serene Jones focuses on the psalms as a resource for testifying and witnessing to experiences of trauma in people's lives. Even though she addresses how the psalms meet those who have endured communal experiences of violence, her insistence that these prayers attend to physical as well as emotional and spiritual pain[11] applies to what the psalms offer those who live with serious illness as well.

It is the lament psalms in particular that both Jones and Deborah Hunsinger set in conversation with a range of traumatic experiences. Even those who are familiar with the psalms may not realize that there are sixty psalms of lament—that's *40 percent* of the entire Psalter. These dozens of lament psalms (as well as the laments of Job, Jeremiah, and beyond) provide spaces of last refuge for those who feel acutely that a sense of hope and despair hang in the balance.[12] That lament psalms make up a sizable minority of prayers in the book of Psalms is also strong evidence that lamenting to God is understood to be a faithful practice—and, therefore, a positive coping strategy. This point needs to be made loudly and clearly. Not only do lament psalms offer those undone by illness language to represent how bodies keep the score of the physical and nonphysical wounds of illness; they also make space for bringing the awfulness of these experiences before God.

Billman and Migliore note that only a minority of lament psalms are penitential in nature; that is, they explicitly link the suffering of the ones praying to their own individual or communal sin (Pss. 6, 32, 38, 51, 102, 130, and 143). Interestingly the penitential lament psalms are the ones most often used in Christian worship. The majority of lament psalms, in contrast, implicitly or explicitly reject the idea that all suffering is traceable to human sin. Far more frequently laments to God in the psalms are motivated by sickness, misfortune, and personal and communal distress.[13] I appreciate and applaud Billman and Migliore's urging Christians to move beyond the more insistent moral frameworks of the penitential lament psalms. At the same time, several of these psalms include powerful language about illness that makes them worth examining here. And close examination reveals that even as linkages between illness and sin are made, such connections are also interrupted by stanzas that refuse to adhere to such tidy logic.

Let's look first at Psalm 38, where struggling with a very ill body likely inspires the graphic physical language of this psalm. The speaker laments, "There is no soundness in my flesh. . . . there is no health in my bones" (v. 3). While there is debate about whether the language of this psalm is intended to be literal or metaphorical,[14] biblical scholar Frederick Gaiser suggests that there is no reason to suspect that the language is merely metaphorical. Physical illness was more prominent in ancient Israel than it is today, and the supplicant's distress may well be manifesting itself in physical ways. At the same time, the poetical and metaphorical rendering of the prayers opens up space for multiple interpretations of the lack of soundness or health in the body.

The psalmist's poetic rendering of the anguish related to being seriously ill also supports the vision of living with cancer that has been set forth in previous chapters: that illness's toll on the body affects not just the body but one's entire sense of self. Gaiser points out how the discussion of "flesh" and "bones" is used elsewhere in the Old Testament (cf. Gen. 2 and Job 10:11) to describe the whole person. The psalmist's lament in Psalm 38, then, testifies to the reality that "illness affects the person, inside and out, flesh and bones, body and spirit."[15]

The psalm is characterized as a penitential psalm because it links the speaker's illness to God's indignation as well as to the speaker's own sin (vv. 2–3). Ancient Israelites struggled to understand illness within a moral framework, insisting that because God is somehow involved in illness, suffering must somehow be the result of sin. This also means, Gaiser suggests, that the Israelites viewed illness as "a time of reflection, of searching for meaning, examining relationships, exploring theology, and actively seeking release. This is especially true, no doubt, in cases of illness where there is no clear and simple treatment."[16] In this particular psalm, the speaker tries out various attempts to explain the illness: it's brought on by God; it's caused by the speaker's own sin or foolishness. These explanations represent attempts to make sense of the illness.

At the same time, it's also important to notice where the psalmist—consumed by the bodily toll the illness is taking—moves beyond a tidy explanation for why the suffering is so extreme:

For my loins are filled with burning,
   and there is no soundness in my flesh.
I am utterly spent and crushed;
   I groan because of the tumult of my heart.
                                            (Ps. 38:7–8)

The physical symptoms described throughout the psalm remain intimately connected with the emotional and spiritual tumult brought on by the illness. Just as researchers of illness-related trauma demonstrate that the body keeps score through experiences of hyperarousal, nightmares, and other intensely embodied reactions to being threatened from within by serious illness, so too does Psalm 38 reflect this reality.

That the body keeps the score for those who are seriously ill often has significant ramifications for the ill person's relationships with others. Recall Christian Wiman's unnerving description of sitting there, "a little skeletal constriction of self—of disappearing self—watching everyone you love . . . drift farther and farther away."[17] The supplicant in Psalm 38 reflects precisely this kind of isolation that accompanies such disorienting pain in the body-self: "My friends and companions stand aloof from my affliction, and my neighbors stand far off" (v. 11). Using the same Hebrew root (*rq*) to talk about the distance illness creates between the one who is sick and the other people in their life, the psalmist appeals to God: "Do not be far from me . . . O LORD, my salvation" (vv. 21–22).[18] The plea is that even when illness creates unbridgeable distance between ourselves and those we love, God will remain close.

In wrestling with the psalm's portrayal of illness as generated by the sufferer's own sin, Gaiser reflects on how he addresses this issue with his students, most of whom are planning to become ministers. He admits that many seminarians balk at using this psalm with those who are ill out of concern for reinforcing the ideas that the illness is their fault, that God is against them, and that they are alone. Gaiser responds by proposing that "the psalms are more primal, more experiential" than a view that insists a singular psalm is *prescriptive* rather than *descriptive* in its attempts to make sense of illness.

Instead he proposes that Psalm 38 provides insight into what happens (i.e., its descriptive function) when someone is forced to endure the indignities of a very ill body; these experiences often prompt spiritual reflection—even a spiritual crisis—on how to make sense of the pain and suffering and on how such attempts also vary depending on the day, even the hour.[19] So lament psalms offer language for those undone by illness to talk about not just their physical pain but also the traumatic emotional, psychic, and spiritual wounds that remain imprinted on the body for years, sometimes for the remainder of their lives.

Lament psalms are helpful not just because they provide language that takes us into the neighborhood of trauma but also because they petition and cry out to God as the One who witnesses trauma, a God who, the psalmist testifies, will answer and save (38:15, 22). Prayers like Psalm 38 move through a full range of emotions—anguish, grief, despair, trust, and hope—creating what Jones calls a "vivid imaginative space" for the speaker to "actively inhabit the language" that describes aspects of the trauma.[20] This practice can also be understood as an example of what psychologists call "positive religious coping" as it opens avenues for those traumatized by their illness to move in the direction of adapting to the circumstances of being seriously ill.

Although Jones resists a tidy telling of the biblical story that bends toward resolution, when she reads theologian John Calvin's commentary on the psalms alongside Judith Herman's insights about recovery from trauma, she proposes that inhabiting the language of the psalms helps assure the ones praying that "God is in control and that they are protected and heard by God." Furthermore, psalms that speak of God's deliverance from the suffering create space where those who have experienced traumatic violence can once again imagine themselves as agents who have some control over the world they inhabit.[21]

For all of Jones's insistence on highlighting for those who live with trauma the ways in which the biblical narrative resists a tidy, nomic structure, her reliance on Calvin seems at times to steer her toward confident affirmations that God is in control, even of the trauma-saturated parts of our world. While such strong claims are no doubt reassuring to many, it is also possible that such confident affirmations of God's providence may lead those who live in the aftermath of trauma to struggle with the dissonance between their experiences of being undone alongside the insistence that a loving, benevolent God is always in control.

Perhaps because he addresses more directly the internal threat from which those who are ill are often unable to create distance, Gaiser's assessment of the help offered by Psalm 38 is more tempered than Jones's, mellowed by the sense of ongoingness for those who suffer from serious illness or other chronic conditions. That the psalm ends in hope, trusting in God, "my salvation," Gaiser notes, suggests that the speaker imposes some sense of nomos on the experience of illness. But is this attempt at ordering enough? Gaiser wonders. He acknowledges that this psalm (like all psalms) is meant to be used in worship and that the structure provided by rituals of liturgy and prayer offer frameworks of meaning that facilitate coping with illness by mitigating the sense of anomie so often experienced by those whose bodies keep the score of illness-related trauma.

At the same time, the taming of the chaos enacted by the movement from the beginning of Psalm 38 to its end is "neither final nor complete," Gaiser suggests.[22] For so many living with cancer and other diseases, illness continues. That religious coping by those with cancer fluctuates between positive and negative coping strategies over the course of diagnosis, treatment, and beyond[23] connects to the movement in the psalms from lament to praise, back to lament once again.

Another penitential lament psalm that includes vivid descriptions of the embodied experience of being seriously ill is Psalm 6:

Be gracious to me, O LORD, for I am languishing;
   O LORD, heal me, for my bones are shaking with terror.
My soul also is struck with terror
   while you, O LORD—how long?

(Ps. 6:2–3)

The prayer immediately presents illness as more than just a physical issue, one that is also intensely emotional and spiritual. This particular lament psalm follows the common pattern of pointing in three directions at once: toward God, self, and others. The existence of this threefold cry draws attention, Gaiser suggests, to the "complexity and causality of illness." The psalm begins with the supplicant asking God not to rebuke in anger or discipline in wrath. In other words, the speaker is saying, "Somehow God is *in* my illness, as am I, and as are others around me, for good or for ill."[24]

Even as some space is devoted in the psalm to contemplating the reasons for the speaker's illness—maybe it's divine anger, maybe divine discipline—once again there are other parts of the psalm that leave the question of fault aside and capture in starkly physical terms what it's like to become undone, very possibly by a physical illness:

> I am weary with my moaning;
> 	every night I flood my bed with tears;
> 	I drench my couch with my weeping.
> My eyes waste away because of grief.
> 	(Ps. 6:6–7)

The speaker expresses terror over what's happening to the body-self and wants to know where and how God is present amid this awful undoing of the body that is also an undoing of the self. The psalmist petitions God to turn—not just to regard the psalmist's condition—but to offer salvation and deliverance from illness (v. 4). The psalm concludes with words of consolation: the Lord has heard the supplicant's weeping and accepts the prayer. The concluding verses can be read as testimony of the psalmist's healing. The psalm begins with a direct request of God: *Heal me*, and ends with an affirmation that God has heard the prayer. The movement in the psalms from lament to confidence and praise is not merely adherence to a liturgical formula, Gaiser insists, but witness to the real experience of healing.[25] Those who are ill become well. Healing does happen.

Yet we all know that healing doesn't always happen. The speaker's concluding words in Psalm 6 could also express a confidence in God's presence and responsiveness amid the illness. Gaiser admits that we are kept in the dark about the nature and extent of the healing. I know that for me, even though "my" cancer is incurable, being able to have several years of remission has permitted me to move from "eyes wast[ing] away because of grief" (v. 7) to confessing, "The LORD has heard my supplication" (v. 9). But living with incurable cancer often means that movement toward thankfulness for the healing that's taken place may well be replaced again by lament for the resurgence of the illness.

Those who live with serious illnesses like cancer may take solace in a variety of psalms, whether or not they specifically reference illness. One psalm that deserves more attention in conversations about lament and making space for being undone by trauma is Psalm 88, perhaps the most irresolute of all psalms. The psalmist's "soul is full of troubles" (v. 3), buried under the weight of isolation brought on by psychic, spiritual, and emotional distress. The speaker petitions God repeatedly, pleading for some sign of divine responsiveness:

> But I, O LORD, cry out to you;
>   in the morning my prayer comes before you.
> O LORD, why do you cast me off?
>   Why do you hide your face from me?
>   (Ps. 88:13–14)

Interrogations of God, accompanied by accusations of divine unresponsiveness and absence, appear in Psalm 88 as they do throughout the lament psalms. This calling God to account emerges in response to testimony throughout the biblical narrative that the character of God is One who will always be present, without fail. As the writer of Exodus attests,

"The LORD, the LORD,
a God merciful and gracious,
slow to anger,
and abounding in steadfast love and faithfulness,
keeping steadfast love for the thousandth generation."
(Exod. 34:6–7)

The speaker in Psalm 88 challenges God to be the God of Israel reflected in Exodus 34, the One who loves and cares for God's people. But unlike most other lament psalms, Psalm 88 ends not with a hopeful proclamation of being heard by God but in despair. The psalmist communicates a sense of utter isolation, with darkness as the speaker's only companion.

Interpreters of this psalm also suggest that the speaker appears close to death, a state described in physical terms, with eyes growing "dim through sorrow" (v. 9). The insistent questioning of God throughout the psalm indicts any attempt to package the supplicant's suffering in a tidy framework, moral or otherwise. Why such suffering? Why doesn't God respond? The questions hang suspended, unanswered.

Theologian Kathryn Greene-McCreight meditates on this psalm in the context of her own experience of living with life-threatening mental illness. While living with diseases like cancer differs in significant ways from living with mental illness, there are also important moments of overlap, commonalities that become apparent when this psalm is read as a psalm about someone who is seriously ill. Greene-McCreight's important insight about being ill is appropriate for those living with cancer as well: "Sick people are not necessarily weak," she writes. "I am ashamed to admit I did not already know this. Sick people are afflicted."[26] To be ill is to be afflicted not only physically but also with the disintegration of previously held theological frameworks and even, as this psalm profoundly attests, by the acute experience of the absence of God.

Even though experiences of the absence of God fill the prayers of the psalms and are so ubiquitous that even Jesus himself cannot avoid them, this particular kind of affliction often fails to get the theological or pastoral attention it deserves. Pastoral theologian Piet Zuidgeest's work with those who are grieving leads him to call for a retrieval of religious experiences of God's absence and their reintegration into Christian theology and practice.[27] Indeed, Zuidgeest rightly indicates that biblical testimony of human beings' relationship to God illustrates that the experience of God's absence is much more than a momentary phenomenon for those who are struggling. Rather God's "presence is in the nature of absence."[28] From Solomon's testimony in 1 Kings 8:12 that God dwells "in thick darkness" to the lament in Psalm 88 over the hiddenness of God's face (v. 14), the people of God give voice to those anguished experiences of God's apparent silence over suffering that we so wish were not a part of our lives.

Greene-McCreight casts in stark terms what it's like to live with serious mental illness amid a sense of God's absence. She also witnesses to ways the body keeps the score of depression: "When I am depressed, every thought, every breath, every conscious moment hurts."[29] While not all persons living with serious illnesses like cancer experience depression, studies that focus on illness-related trauma highlight the psychic distress that often accompanies illnesses like cancer and also, often, goes untreated. My visit with the cancer counselor after crying my way through an oncology appointment led to a diagnosis of illness-related depression, confirmation of one of the ways trauma was making itself known in my life with cancer.

That Greene-McCreight finds space within this psalm for her many years of living with mental illness allows her to realize that "despair can live with Christian faith."[30] This insight is a gift to those whose suffering leads them to court despair. One's relationship with God can encompass even such embodied experiences of hopelessness. How, then, might we mitigate ways in which the body keeps score of illness-related trauma? Greene-McCreight describes her strategy for dealing with episodes of serious depression: she resorts to becoming intensely busy in order to avoid having to experience the bodily hurt that each breath brings. Being seriously ill with cancer, however, often means that busying oneself physically is difficult, if not impossible. When those afflicted with cancer are reduced to skeletal selves—to living, breathing, human beings unable to do much more than be "undead"—it becomes exceedingly difficult to avoid experiencing the pain of each conscious moment.

Todd Billings writes about his own embodied practice of reciting the psalms that helped him counteract the ways his body keeps score of the trauma related to his diagnosis.[31] Up front about his weariness in trusting and hoping in God's providential care, Billings finds in the psalms not just space for lament but also for repeated witness to the trustworthiness of God, even when God's actions remain a mystery. Billings not only takes refuge in the lament psalms, but he also recounts a practice of reciting Psalm 27, a psalm of thanksgiving that affirms, "The LORD is my light and my salvation" (v. 1) and asks "to live in the house of the LORD all the days of [his] life"(v. 4). What is striking about Billings's description of saying the words of this psalm is what happened to his body-self when he did so. He would lie down on his living room floor and repeat the words of the psalm. Billings admits praying the words of this psalm "was hard work."[32] But in reciting them over and over again, his "mind would focus, tense muscles would release, and [he] was brought into a place that was not just the story of [his] cancer, [his] steroids, [his] chemo."

The words of Psalm 27 bring Billings into a wider space— the expansive space of God's story—and help him reframe his life in ways that move him toward trust, even hope:[33]

> I believe that I shall see the goodness of the LORD
>   in the land of the living.
> Wait for the LORD
>   be strong, and let you heart take courage.
>   (Ps. 27:13–14)

The psalms offer Billings space to lament his body, compromised by cancer, as well as the emotional and spiritual challenges his journey with cancer presents while also helping him "reshape his heart" to trust again in the care of God.

Billings's description offers a poignant example of the ways in which praying the psalms can counteract how the body keeps score of illness-related trauma. As trauma research demonstrates, trauma leaves an imprint on the mind, brain, and body, but treatment for trauma has not always taken seriously enough the role of the body in addressing it. Even though trauma researcher Bessel van der Kolk does not dismiss talk therapy as a helpful tool in addressing trauma, he has become more convinced that practices that facilitate healing from trauma must be practices that allow those who live with trauma to integrate sense experiences and "live with the natural flow of feeling" within the body.[34] Billings's embodied practice of repeating the words of the psalm until his body relaxes seems to have had this kind of bodily effect.

Billings also talks about how reciting psalms helps him embody and embrace thanksgiving for God's continued *hesed*— God's covenantal, steadfast love and faithfulness—even when God's absence is more strongly felt than God's presence. Billings insists that the psalms are valuable not simply because they offer language for how the body keeps the score. Even more important, they make space for his anguish at the suffering that cancer forces on his life. He trusts that God's story—in all its mystery and paradox—is a story that provides nomos even when our individual or collective human stories do not. Stepping into the structure of the psalms helps relieve some of the pressure Billings feels to make meaning out of his illness. Instead of clarity about the *why* of his illness, Billings discovers a more powerful counternarrative in the psalms, a narrative that doesn't provide answers but instead offers consolation—even relief—to the body-self, even when the threat of cancer remains relentless.

Praying the psalms also opens up pathways for those living with serious illness to see themselves as more than simply victims of the disease. Praying the psalms gives voice to the intense connection we experience between the disease in our bodies and the inner turmoil of the heart. Praying the psalms gives voice to the protest, anger, and grief that accompany life with serious illness, but it does so within the larger context of a relationship to the God who hears and responds to such anguished prayers. As Hunsinger suggests, lament keeps the channels open between God and the sufferer. By doing so, lament can open a way for the unendurable to be endured.[35]

Space in the Story of Job for Illness-Related Trauma

The last two chapters have explored the persistent pressure on those living with cancer to tell a palatable, meaningful, and hope-filled cancer story. Barbara Ehrenreich's narrative makes visible how much resistance there can be to stories that open up space for the anger and sadness of having to live with serious illness. Incorporating the language of trauma can enable more robust communication of the breadth and depth of the suffering for those who are seriously ill. The vocabulary of trauma emphasizes the emotional, psychic, and spiritual suffering that accompany life with serious illness and helps one avoid capitulating to pressure to tell a tidy, logical story.

In the ancient world of the Old Testament, the dominant nomic story for why people suffer promoted the view that suffering was a punishment for sin. Ancient Israelites believed that those who are righteous are blessed by God while those who are wicked receive their just deserts of suffering. Enter the book of Job, a story of a righteous man who loses almost everything precious to him—his children, his health, and his possessions. The story's plot flies in the face of Israel's go-to explanations for suffering. Thus the pressing question for Job, as well as for readers and hearers of this story in both the ancient and contemporary world, is "What happens when go-to explanations are not up to the task of explaining undeserved suffering?"

I suggested earlier that for many of us living with cancer and other serious illnesses, the insistent question tends less to be "Why this suffering?" than "How?": "How will I live in the face of cancer threatening to claim my life?" If this is the case, why spend time on the why question? Jason Micheli, a pastor recently diagnosed with incurable mantle-cell lymphoma, offers a response. He admits that despite finding the why question unhelpful and unproductive, he nevertheless has been unable to avoid periods of asking, "Why is God doing this to me?" even as he assures himself that he doesn't believe God is doing it to him.[36] Micheli speaks for more than just himself when he insists that even when why is not the primary, animating question of living with cancer, it's a question that's almost impossible to avoid.

In a religious context, the why question gets enveloped within the "theodicy" question. *Theodicy* is a term made up of two Greek words: *theos* — God, and *dike* — justice. It addresses possible ways to make sense of how and why a just God would allow the suffering of the innocent. Even though the word has theological roots, the concept of theodicy also stretches beyond narrower attempts at justifying God in the face of seemingly inexplicable suffering. Every story about a meaningful world also has a theodicy, a workable explanation of meaning and coherence in the face of aspects that fail to make sense. The task of theodicy, sociologist of religion Peter Berger observes, is not necessarily to solve a logical problem but to repair an imperiled worldview. And it is in this drive to repair a threatened worldview, Berger cautions, that theodicy can end up supporting explanations that should not be supported.[37]

Indeed. Recall Ehrenreich's repeated encounter with theodicies that render cancer a "can't-miss opportunity" to become a better person or Bowler's encounter with the theodicy that undergirds her neighbor's insistence that there must be a logical explanation for her cancer. It's not hard to find examples of (often problematic, inadequate) ways that we try to make sense of suffering that upends our sense of a meaningful world.

And then there's the book of Job, a book countless persons have turned to for insight into the theodicy question. Various characters in the story try on possible answers to the riddle of why Job suffers. What I find most intriguing and helpful about the story of Job, however, especially when it's placed in conversation with the kind of stories we tell about those who are seriously ill, is the way in which it can be interpreted as an *anti*theodicy. Rather than answering the question of God's justice related to Job's suffering, the story offers something else: a realistic story about Job's undoneness that refuses to validate tidy explanations for his suffering and, in the end, opens a way to continue on in the aftermath of great suffering, even when answers are not forthcoming.

To say that the book of Job offers a dose of realism does not mean that it's an easily understood story. On the contrary: it is a complex and, at times, a vexing book. The story is set in the land of Uz, a place not locatable on a map. The character of Job seems to represent the ideal righteous man, with the narrator repeatedly emphasizing Job's blamelessness, making it eminently clear that the suffering visited upon him is "not due to any sin of his, known or unknown."[38]

Following the introduction of Job, the plot shifts to a heavenly court occupied by God, angels, and a character called Satan. In Hebrew the word *satan* refers to an "accuser" or "adversary," a prosecuting attorney of sorts who investigates the details of a prosecution and brings them to God's attention.[39] In God's conversation with the adversary, there is reference again to Job's impeccable credentials as blameless and upright (1:8). But the adversary challenges God, predicting that if Job loses the blessings of his life, he will curse God. God takes up the challenge, allowing the adversary to take what Job has away from him.

The scene shifts back to Job just as he learns that his livestock, his servants, and his children have all been killed. Job responds by worshiping God: "'The LORD gave, and the LORD has taken away; blessed be the name of the LORD'" (1:21). Just in case readers fail to absorb the point, the narrator emphasizes again that even when he's tested, Job neither sins nor charges God with any wrongdoing (1:22). The next scene returns to the heavenly court where God again extols Job's blamelessness and righteousness, pointing out that even amid his grief over losing so much, Job "'still persists in his integrity'" (2:3). But the adversary goads God on, wagering that if God touches Job's "'bone and his flesh'" (2:5), he won't be able to endure it; he'll end up cursing God. Disturbingly, God acquiesces to the adversary, permitting him to further afflict Job. The adversary then causes painful sores to cover Job's body. At this point, Job's wife, who has also shared in the traumatic loss of children, servants, and livestock, is bitter. "'Curse God and die,'" she urges him (2:9). But Job rebukes her, calling her "'foolish'" for questioning God (2:10).

The book of Job's depiction of the tension between spouses in the aftermath of traumatic events like serious illness reflects the challenges many couples face. It's not just Job who's undone over losing his children, his health, and his property; clearly (understandably!) his wife is undone as well. But in the immediate aftermath of such great losses, the spouses respond in radically different ways. Job's wife expresses her grief through anger and bitterness directed at God while Job seems invested in a faith that doesn't question God after such an awful turn of events. Many of us living with serious illnesses and other traumas likely recognize such disparate responses between ourselves and our partners to our suddenly changed lives. Just like Job and his wife, my husband and I often seemed to be in different emotional places, especially in those early days after my diagnosis. It was like we were on a seesaw—one was up, and the other was down. And whenever one of us would start to move up, out of the valley of the shadow, the other would sink down, back into the valley, until it was time to switch places once again.

What's noteworthy about this exchange between Job and his wife in the early days of their trauma is that although Job initially rejects his wife's proposal for how to cope, it's not long before Job comes to embrace a stance very similar to his wife's. A few verses after Job rebukes his wife, he comes to curse the day he was born (3:1–3), and in the chapters that follow he questions God repeatedly.[40] As is often the case in ancient and biblical narratives, Job's wife fades from the story, and we are unable to learn more about how their relationship progresses, whether they eventually get on the same emotional page, or if she moves on to other ways of coping as he comes to occupy a more anguished place.

After Job's exchange with his wife, the story shifts to the longest scene of the book. The narrator reports that Job's friends learn of his troubles and set out "to console and comfort him" (2:11). What happens next is reminiscent of a scene many of us who become afflicted with serious illness know well: when the friends approach Job, they fail to recognize him (2:12). The defining physical characteristics of Job that his friends knew and loved have faded from view to such an extent that they are shocked to realize that the man they see is, in fact, their friend. Face-to-face with the toll Job's calamities have exacted on his body and his spirit, the friends are moved to tears; they tear their robes and cover their heads with dust, both expressions of grief in the ancient world. The friends then sit with him for seven days and nights, evoking images of the Jewish ritual of sitting shivah, a practice done in the presence of the body of someone who has died.[41] His friends do this, the narrator tells us, because they "saw that his suffering was very great" (2:13).

That Job's friends initially treat his acute suffering over multiple sources of trauma—the loss of children, health, servants, and animals—as a death hearkens back to Shelly Rambo's description of living with trauma: "The challenge for those who experience trauma is to move in a world in which the boundaries and parameters of life no longer seem to hold, to provide meaning."[42] The friends' sitting shivah with Job acknowledges the trauma Job experiences. For the first week they are with him, they do not try to explain or make sense of the awfulness; they simply occupy that traumatic space with him where death and life no longer exist in opposition. After seven days, however, Job finds his voice and tries to put words to what he's experiencing, and at this point the book shifts from prose to poetry. The tenor of Job's poetic cursing of the day he was born parallels one of the testimonies found by Susan Gubar from another woman who survived debulking surgery: "I'd rather be dead." The third chapter of the book of Job contains poignant testimony by Job of being utterly undone by all he's been through. He longs for death, but it doesn't come; he craves rest but finds none.

Similar to Ehrenreich's stubborn refusal to tell the much-rehearsed story about how cancer is helping her build character,

Job's insistence on expressing his grief in an honest way also provokes strong reactions from his friends. Ehrenreich's expressions of anger over being diagnosed with cancer make others uncomfortable, and Job's friends rail against his expressions of grief, clinging tightly instead to belief in a nomic universe that operates according to particular moral laws of justice and retribution. In their minds, his experiences of such grave suffering must mean that he is somehow responsible for it.

Job's friend Eliphaz is sure Job must have sinned to bring such suffering upon himself. He implores Job, "'Think now, who that was innocent ever perished? Or where were the upright cut off?'" (4:7) As Job puts words to the anguish he's experiencing, his friend Bildad spends his time defending God. "'Does God pervert justice?'" he asks. "'If you are pure and upright, surely then he will . . . restore you to your rightful place" (8:3, 6). Finally his friend Zophar takes the position of what interpreters often call "the philosopher."[43] He reminds Job that his fate is in his own hands: "'If you direct your heart rightly,'" Zophar tells Job, "'you will stretch out your hands toward him'" and "'forget your misery'" (11:13, 16). The friends are insistent: Job's suffering, somehow, has to be able to be crammed within the boundaries of the laws of a moral universe.

But Job refuses to stand for his friends' attempts to explain his suffering, insisting instead on talking about the toll these traumatic experiences are taking on him. In powerful poetic cadence, Job recounts his months of emptiness and nights of misery, insisting that he will speak the "'anguish of [his] spirit'" (7:11)—an anguish that afflicts his body as well. He laments that God is passing him by. His speech is full of questions about why God has abandoned him. Like the speaker in Psalm 88, Job reminds God that a central aspect of God's character is protection of the innocent and defense of the defenseless.[44]

Job's arguing with his friends goes on for over two dozen chapters. As biblical scholar James Kugel notes, Job's friends doggedly repeat stories about why bad things happen that reflect the convictions of the wider society of the ancient world. Kugel, who has lived his own version of the cancer story, observes, "[b]ut Job is really suffering. For him, this debate is not primarily about ideas but about what is happening to him, the ruin of his body day after day."[45] Job pushes back against the friends' repeated appeals to logical reasons why his life has become undone.

> "I loathe my life;
> I will give free utterance to my complaint;
> I will speak in the bitterness of my soul."
>
> (Job 10:1)

He repeatedly tells them, "'I am not inferior to you'" (12:3; 13:2) for refusing to talk about his afflictions in ways that endorse the logic of the worldviews they are invested in. Just as Ehrenreich refuses to give in to the pressure to tell a positive, uplifting story about her life with breast cancer, so Job resolutely makes space for his testimony about the suffering that remains—the physical, psychic, and spiritual suffering over why someone as upright as he would be visited by such awfulness. He is determined to speak "'the bitterness of [his] soul'" (10:1).

Many commentaries on the book of Job make clear that Job's friends don't really behave like friends. His "friends'" support for him in his pain quickly morphs into long speeches of challenge and judgment of Job's telling of his own story. Job's challenges with his friends links to Kathryn's pithy reflection of what she wished she had known when she was diagnosed with basil-cell carcinoma at age forty-five: that she would lose friends. "Dealing with cancer was enough without the drama of worrying about friends and family members who could not deal with my cancer," she laments.[46] The story of Job provides ample illustrations of the ways in which friends can at times make it harder to tell realistic cancer stories that include space for the trauma and experiences of despair, isolation, and meaninglessness.

In considering how the story of Job illumines ways to care—and not to care—for those undone by trauma, Deborah Hunsinger makes an insightful connection between the behavior of Job's friends and the role of caregivers for those who live with persistent emotional, psychic, and spiritual suffering. Caregivers, she writes, "aren't there to explain the origin of suffering, as Job's friends sought to do, or to minimize its impact. They are there simply to share it and to convey it to God."[47] Those who live with the aftereffects of illness-related trauma need the support of others who allow room for expressions of what it's like to be undone by illness.

That fact that Job's friends' attempts to explain his suffering seem to lead to more suffering for Job also points to an important insight about what it means to be a friend. The dynamic between Job and his friends, theologian Daniel Castelo has noted, illustrates that "friendship is a serious moral-spiritual activity that has great potential for ill or good, especially in terms of suffering and pain."[48] In contrast to the behavior of Job's friends, Castelo proposes that the Christian practice of loving our neighbor as ourselves may well mean that when we sit with those who suffer we attend to matters *other than* theological explanations for their suffering. In situations of extreme suffering, our befriending needs to take the form of "gentleness, long-suffering, steadfastness, loyalty, and devotion," all characteristics common to Christ's embodiment of friendship.[49]

Rather than letting his friends dictate the terms of the debate as to why his life has unraveled, Job turns instead to God to "'argue [his] case'" (13:3). In his final speech in chapters 29–31, his attention to the friends and their arguments fades into the background. He presses God to let him know where he strayed, to point out what he possibly could have done to deserve all this suffering. In contrast to the friends who talk *about* God, Job insists on talking *to* God. The climax of the book then comes when God addresses Job "out of the whirlwind" (38:1). It's important to acknowledge up front that God's response from the whirlwind is not an *explanation* for Job's suffering. Instead God questions Job. "'Where were you when I laid the foundation of the earth?'" (38:4). What transpires between God and Job is neither what Job nor the readers of Job expect. God's response does not address Job's many questions, and just how God's response (and Job's response to God) should be interpreted continues to be debated. Is God merely chiding Job for being a mere human while God is Lord of all?

While some interpreters suggest that God mocks Job for his hubris in demanding an answer for his suffering from the Creator of the universe, others take a different approach. They note that God's speech is not rational discourse; in other words, God refuses to engage Job's line of reasoning. God offers a poetic nonanswer that speaks instead of God's providence over all creation. God's speech, Thomas Long suggests, is a divine rejection of imposing human concepts of a moral order upon God.[50]

Job responds with a kind of humility he hasn't shown since the beginning of the book: "'I am of small account; what shall I answer you?'" (40:4) Job's response is followed by God's speaking out of the whirlwind a second time in a speech that seems even more harsh and mocking. God insists on interrogating Job about his questioning the justice of God: "'Will you condemn me that you may be justified?'" (40:8). This divine speech also contains cryptic references to two mythical monsters, Behemoth and Leviathan, and illustrations about how they were created by God just as Job was. Pastor Michael Thompson suggests that the monsters' reputation for evil helps emphasize that God is in control of every part of creation, even parts that are considered evil.[51] One of the reasons for the litany of questions for Job in both divine speeches, it seems, is to point out not only that Job doesn't understand divine activity but that there's much divine activity of which Job is not even aware.

Job's final response to God is brief. Not only has Job heard God speak, but Job has seen God (42:5). If readers were hoping the book of Job would answer the theodicy question once and for all, they are likely disappointed. But as Thompson observes, the concluding chapters of Job shift the focus from theodicy to *theophany*, to the appearance of God to the one who is suffering.[52] Job cries out repeatedly to God, and in the end Job is answered not by an explanation but by an encounter with the Divine. Job responds to this encounter by insisting that he will "'repent in dust and ashes'" (42:6), an act of accepting his smallness before God.

But the book does not end there. In the final verses, God takes Job's friends to task for not speaking the truth about God and suffering. Even though God does not offer a rational explanation for undeserved suffering, God issues a definitive rejection of theodicies that say suffering is always explainable, always linked to sin. In fact, theologian David Burrell proposes that the inclusion of the book of Job in the Hebrew biblical canon represents a challenge to conventional human attempts at coming up with arguments that explain why suffering happens.[53] Following Burrell, we might say that the book of Job presents a stark challenge to conventional cancer story lines that talk about how living with cancer is necessarily personally and spiritually edifying, or that it has to be viewed as a great opportunity to grow closer to God. The fact that the book of Job is dominated by Job's protests against God opens space for those undone by cancer to cry out against their experience of being undone as well.

Job's vindication before his friends, however, is *still* not the end of the story. The final passage of the book returns to the plotline from the beginning of the story where God is responsible for taking away all that Job has. In this final chapter, the narrator reports that God restores the fortunes of Job (42:10). Not only does Job get back what was taken from him, but he ends up with even more than he had before, even to the point of bringing new children into the world. Just as readers come to terms with the irresolution present in God's response from the whirlwind to Job, we are thrust back into a framework where Job seems to get his just deserts. He passed the divine test and is rewarded.

On one level, it seems that an all's-well-that-ends-well conclusion imposes a strong sense of nomos on the story. Some may conclude that Job struggles for a while with the meaning of suffering but then moves past the struggle into a life that once again makes sense. Before we move in that direction, however, it is important to consider what is and is not in the story. For starters, while we hear that Job is given "twice as much as he had before" (42:10), including the same number of children he and his wife had had before tragedy struck, there's no mention of his wife in this final scene. We may want to chalk this up to the supporting role typically played by women in ancient writings; it's possible that the book's author finds it unnecessary to comment on her abiding presence. But it also raises some interesting questions, like whether or not the restoration of Job's fortunes includes his wife.

It's no secret that weathering traumatic events like serious illnesses is often hard on a marriage. One study of cancer patients indicates that a majority of marriages (65 percent) dealing with the cancer of one spouse report having a closer relationship after the cancer diagnosis.[54] While this might seem encouraging, these findings also highlight that a sizable minority of couples *do not* experience a heightened sense of intimacy. And in our contemporary context, when the spouse with cancer is female, the likelihood of divorce increases sevenfold.[55] Job and his wife, however, hail from a different time and place. Nevertheless, the absence of Job's wife from these final scenes provides an opening to contemplate whether or how their relationship survived the trauma that filled their lives.

What, then, are we to make of Job's puzzling reversal of fortune? One compelling reading of the ending of the book of Job comes from biblical scholar Carol Newsom. She argues that because the prose ending of Job's getting back what he lost and more comes *after* the conversations between God and Job, its meaning is different from what it would be if there had been no intervening dialogue between Job and the Divine. That the restoration of Job's life follows his dialogue with God moves it into the realm of the tragic, into a world where awful things happen and we can't comprehend why. Newsom compares the Job of the final scene to the ostrich in the divine speech (39:13–18). Just like the ostrich, Job brings children into a dangerous world where they could be crushed and trampled (cf. 39:15). While the ostrich forgets the world's dangers, however, it's highly unlikely, given what Job has been through, that he could forget the vulnerability that accompanies any human life.

"But what of the ostrich's laughter?" Newsom asks. In the divine speech, the ostrich, the wild ass, and Leviathan all laugh defiantly because, as she suggests, they all lack the capacity for tragedy. But Job is a man who has experienced traumatic losses in spades; a man who encounters God but doesn't emerge with answers to his questions; and yet a man who nevertheless remains in relationship with the Divine. Job is thus a man who possesses a capacity for tragedy.

Even though he knows that his righteousness does not guarantee protection from the vicissitudes of life, and even though he's hyperaware of the potential fleeting nature of his joy, Job is still, stunningly, capable of laughter. Newsom points out that the narrator includes the "strangely gratuitous information" of Job's new daughters' names, all playful variations on the word "beauty." They "are a form of laughter—not heedless or anarchic laughter—but human and therefore tragic laughter."[56] Job chooses, even at the risk of more suffering, to live and love again. This transformation of Job is not unlike the shift we see repeatedly in the psalms from lament and despair back to praise and thanksgiving.

The book of Job validates the telling of a realistic story about losing one's health and the trauma one experiences because of it. At the same time, the book of Job makes space for realistic cancer stories to include forceful challenges to conventional plots that strive to have it all nicely packaged and following a tidy logic. And perhaps most important, the book of Job models a relationship with the Divine that allows for anger, grief, complaint, and protest, a relationship that may not yield clear answers regarding the reason for suffering but one that can move between tragedy and joy, and one that dares to include laughter even when the risks of living are intimately understood.

Foreclosure of the Future: Why Have You Forsaken Me?

Theologians who attend to the wounds of trauma cannot neglect the trauma that lives at the heart of the Christian story. Those who call themselves Christian, Hunsinger writes, "are indelibly stamped with the unbearable sorrow of this man, Jesus." Not only did he endure an unjust, horrible, shameful death, but his friends denied, betrayed, and abandoned him. How can such a terrible story be borne, especially by those who have endured similar trauma?[57]

This terrible story of the killing of Jesus the Christ is set within the wider drama of the gospel story, a story of the good news of salvation for the world. For Christians, this story is not just an ancient drama of a Jewish man, Jesus, who was born under Roman rule and wandered the countryside preaching the reign of God. It is also a story that lays bare the heart of God as One who enters the world of disease, suffering, and injustice in the person of Jesus Christ only to endure torture and an unjust death, and then, ultimately, to live again. This God is the One who promises new life not just to humanity but to the entire creation.

It's such an important story that the Bible contains four different versions in four different Gospels. While the plots of each of the Gospels drive toward the climactic death and resurrection of Jesus, it's important—especially when focusing on issues of trauma—to consider the movement from Jesus' hope-filled ministry of healing and teaching to the abrupt, traumatic move to the cross. Followers of Jesus see a future opening up where the ill are healed and the invisible in society are made visible. They come to believe that he is the one who will usher in a new political era when there will be enough for those who've never had enough. With Jesus' awful death on a cross, however, it's not only Jesus' own future that is foreclosed but the future of all who understood him to be their Messiah, the one who would bring *shalom*.

The four Gospel stories have much in common, but they also differ from one another in important ways. They tell a story of Jesus' ministry of healing and teaching but also a story of how his ministry gets him into trouble with the authorities. They tell of his betrayal, arrest, and torture. They all make clear that this is a story of *moral* evil; Jesus is sentenced to die by crucifixion, the punishment Roman authorities used for political rebels.

But just two of the four Gospels—Mark and Matthew—include Jesus' anguished cry of abandonment from the cross.

The focus in this section will be on Mark's Gospel, the oldest Gospel, one that scholars working with trauma theory are drawn to in thinking deeply about pain, loss, and trauma. Take, for instance, biblical scholars Maia Kotrosits and Hal Taussig's recent claims that the rawness and creativity of the Gospel of Mark allows it to be a companion for those of us who need to think about "how we might live with and in the wake of loss."[58] As discussed in the previous chapter, the trauma associated with serious illness profoundly affects one's ability to imagine the future. Cancer and other chronic conditions can fracture our imaginations, leaving us anxious and despairing about what's to come. Mark's unsettled narrative lives in that space of a foreclosed future, even as the story refuses to end there. But neither does this Gospel neatly resolve; rather its incomplete and ongoing ending is a place where pain, recovery, failure, and the future all exist in tension with one another.[59]

Mark focuses on three key scenes in Jesus' life: his baptism, transfiguration, and crucifixion. Jesus' baptism by John the Baptist occurs early in chapter 1 (vv. 9–11), a scene that concludes with a voice from heaven declaring, "'You are my Son, the Beloved; with you I am well pleased'" (v. 11). Before the chapter's end, Jesus has begun his ministry, proclaiming "'the good news of God'" that "'the kingdom of God has come near'" (vv. 14–15). A new future is being opened up for those who encounter Jesus. The story testifies to a startling number of healings. Early chapters of Mark overflow with healing stories and reports of Jesus' parabolic teachings.

Mark's story of Jesus, however, is always multiple. Amid the healings and teachings is an undercurrent of opposition to Jesus and his ministry. And even as healing persists throughout the Gospel, those stories are often complicated: Jesus is grabbed unexpectedly by a bleeding woman (5:27) and corrected by a desperate mother whom he insults before healing her daughter (7:24–30). These stories depict pain and healing as intimately intertwined and relationships as containing complicated combinations of both.[60]

Hearers and readers of Mark's Gospel are told right away in chapter 1 about the identity of Jesus as the Son of God. Throughout the Gospel, however, are repeated indications that his identity and mission are misunderstood, even by those closest to him. The story of the transfiguration in Mark 9 stands as the dramatic centerpiece, where Jesus' identity as the Son of God is made known to a wider audience. Jesus takes some disciples with him to a mountaintop, where his body becomes a figure of light. His clothes dazzle; Elijah and Moses appear beside him. Out of the cloud a voice speaks to those gathered on the mountain, "'This is my Son, the Beloved; listen to him!'" (9:7). This second pronouncement of Jesus as the Son of God is meant for others to hear. The voice from the clouds confirms for the disciples that he is the one on whom a new future rests.

While the first ten chapters of Mark span several years of Jesus' life, chapters 11–16 occupy a single week. Just before the story of Jesus' arrest and death begins in Mark 14, chapter 13 offers what interpreters call a "little apocalypse": the foretelling of the destruction of the temple. Most scholars agree that Mark was written around 70 CE, the year of the siege and conquering of Jerusalem and the destruction of the temple. Recent scholarship is paying more attention to the trauma of these events that those in Mark's audience had recently endured.[61] First-century Jewish historian Josephus testifies to the devastation by saying that the war "laid all signs of beauty quite waste."[62] Jews (both Jews who followed Jesus and those who did not) were facing a future of life without the temple or an intact sacred city; it's not surprising, therefore, that Mark's Gospel uses apocalyptic language to describe this trauma-inducing destruction.

The cosmic finale envisioned in this "little apocalypse," interestingly, comes not at the end of Mark but between the cleansing of the temple (11:15–19) and the story of the crucifixion. Using the lens of trauma to interpret the positioning of this passage before the crucifixion and empty tomb, Kostrosits and Taussig propose that its place in the story reflects what those who endure trauma often experience: a profound sense of being changed, of the future foreclosing, while the world continues its steady march into the future, seemingly unchanged. Mark's vision of the end stands in such an ambiguous middle, refusing to be final.[63]

While the Gospel of Mark operates on a political level, it simultaneously tells a more intimate story of the man Jesus, his suffering, and the eclipsing of his own future, along with the future about which he preached. Just as the Psalms and the story of Job witness to how friends can become distant when we endure great suffering, so too do Mark's stories witness to the betrayal and abandonment of Jesus by his friends when he needs them most (14:32–45, 66–72).

Tried, beaten, and mocked, Jesus is brought out to Golgotha and crucified. Mark sets the scene: Jesus is nailed to the cross in the morning, and as he moves closer to death, darkness moves over the land (15:33), symbolizing the difficulty of seeing clearly the meaning of the crucifixion, of the world turning colder with the killing of the Son of God.[64] As death nears, Jesus cries out in a loud voice. Both Mark and Matthew report the cry first in Aramaic: *Eloi, Eloi, lema sabachthani?*; and then, again, in Greek, which translates as "'My God, my God, why have you forsaken me?'" (Matt. 27:45; Mark 15:34). This is the only time Jesus speaks from the cross in Mark, his words heavy with anguish.

Those who were present at the cross, along with the ancient followers of Jesus who hear this cry as part of the gospel story, would have recognized it as the opening lines of the prayer of lament in Psalm 22. Both Mark and Matthew report that those who hear him think he's calling for Elijah, a possible mishearing of the Aramaic *Eloi*. This mishearing reinforces one of the dominant themes of Mark: that Jesus is continually misinterpreted and misunderstood, even by those closest to him.

Jesus cries out one last time and breathes his last. The temple curtain is torn in two, and a third and final time, Mark's story confirms Jesus' identity as the Son of God. This final proclamation comes not from heaven but from the centurion, the one in charge of the day's crucifixions. He's the one who says, "'Truly this man was God's Son!'" (15:39). This statement has engendered significant debate over the centuries; the literal translation from the Greek is "This man is son of God," which could be a reference to Jesus as simply a pious person. At the same time, the way Greek language is structured leads translators to assume a "the" within the sentence. Furthermore, taking symmetry of Mark's Gospel into consideration, it seems likely the declaration of Jesus as *the* Son of God in chapter 1 would be paired with the more definitive declaration by the centurion.[65] If that is the case, the Gospel paints a poignant picture of Jesus' being betrayed and denied by those closest to him, followed by the least likely person at the foot of the cross identifying him as the Son of God.

What are we to make of this cry of dereliction and the violent ending for the Son of God and the future he proclaimed? In contrast to the supplicant of the lament psalms and Job, the human being suffering here is Jesus the Christ, a human being Christians believe to also be divine. While interpreters throughout the long history of Christianity have tried to protect Christ's divinity by arguing against the possibility of divine suffering, biblical scholar Morna Hooker argues that these interpreters "fail to grasp the significance of Mark's picture of Jesus as utterly desolate." Jesus experiences the most desolate experience of a life of faith: the sense of being abandoned by God.[66] While I'm most interested in exploring the significance of these moments in the Christian story that go beyond a moral framework, dominant theological interpretations of this cry include the claim that the anguish Jesus experiences is not simply because of his physical suffering and his sense of being abandoned by his friends and by God but also because of the faith conviction that he bears the weight of human sin on the cross. From the writings of the apostle Paul forward, a central Christian affirmation is that Christ died for our sins (1 Cor. 15:3). This means that sickening aspects of sin correspond to the many sickening aspects of the crucifixion, including this sense of godforsakenness.[67] The agony and death of the Son of God is the centerpiece of the divine drama that carries salvific significance.

In her investigation of the parallels between the passion story and other stories of traumatic violence, Serene Jones notes that just as trauma stories are "unstable and multivoiced," so too are theological interpretations of the cross varied and mutable.[68] She observes in her work with women who live in the aftermath of traumatic violence that the sufferings of Christ elicit varying responses by those who have been traumatized. Even as some can be retraumatized through the retelling of Christ's suffering, others are nourished through their identifications with Christ and his suffering. The bringing together of work on traumatic violence with theologies of the cross highlights one important way to read the two plotlines together.

Christian Wiman presents another way of reading experiences of trauma—this time the trauma brought on by serious illness—and Jesus' cry of abandonment from the cross. Wiman finds that this cry breaks the story open beyond its conventional framework of moral evil. Without discounting sin's role in the crucifixion drama, Wiman proposes that the terror of death— and of Christ's death in particular—bursts the bounds of judgment of sin, moving beyond, into "blankness, meaninglessness."[69]

While contemporary first-world Christians tend to be preoccupied with seeing Jesus' significance primarily as an example for people to follow, Wiman insists what is most "moving" and most "durable" about Jesus are the disruptive, disturbing moments of godforsakenness: "'My God, my God, why have you forsaken me?'" (Matt. 27:45; Mark 15:34). These are the words, Wiman confesses, that make him a Christian. These last words uttered by Christ in both Mark and Matthew are words that elicit more questions, such as "Where is God during Jesus' suffering on the cross?" "Where is God in Jesus' final, agonizing moments?" And perhaps most troubling, "Where is God when Jesus dies?" These are not just questions about God's relationship to Jesus; they are questions about God's relationship to all of us, especially to those who suffer in unbearable ways, whose "Why?" seems to be met with silence.

The sense of anomie in Jesus' cry orients Wiman's understanding of himself as a Christian. He insists that Christians can and should learn from atheists about the absence of God. "If you haven't ever experienced God's absence," Wiman insists, "you haven't been paying attention."[70] Drawing on the reflection of theologian Jürgen Moltmann in his now-classic *The Crucified God*, Wiman is persuaded that the radical nature of Christian faith comes in committing oneself to the crucified God.[71] Wiman catches a glimpse in this irresolvable moment of Christ's godforsakenness of a *more* to life than experiences of suffering and forsakenness facilitated by cancer. Christ's suffering and death confirm for Wiman that human love can reach right into the heart of death, but it is not *merely* human love that touches death. This excess, this *more* of sharing our experiences of suffering and anomie, is the source of Wiman's faith in God, his "bright abyss." Wiman's encounter with Jesus' cry of godforsakenness provokes him to imagine that he is not simply a victim of cancer, that his story doesn't end in isolation, overcome by the solitary nature of his pain. Instead he understands his story of suffering from cancer as being held within the story of God's experiences of bodily suffering in the person of Jesus. Because of Jesus' story, Wiman is able to imagine more to his own story as well.

Mark's narrative, however, does not end with Jesus' agonizing cry and death on the cross, and its concluding verses resist tidy resolution. Two days after he has died, Mary Magdalene, Mary the mother of James, and Salome, three followers of Jesus, go to anoint Jesus' dead body. Mark's depiction of this scene has an ominous air; the women head to the tomb "very early," perhaps to avoid being seen (16:2). They're worried about how they will gain entry to the tomb that is blocked by a "very large" stone (16:3). They arrive to find the stone rolled away, a "small miracle" but also perhaps a worrying sign (have thieves beat them to the body?).[72] Within the tomb they find a young man dressed in white who tells them that the one they seek is not there; that he has been raised. The man encourages the women not to be afraid, to go and tell the disciples that they would see Jesus again in Galilee.

Despite hearing words that would seemingly open the future back up for them, the women's reaction is unexpected. They run out of the tomb, terrified, telling no one. As Jones writes,

And then Mark stops the story. At the very moment when we, as readers of the Gospel, are in need of the greatest relief; at the moment in which we are supposed to witness the event of proclamation that launches Christianity into its future and about how the first people of faith really experienced resurrection—Mark does not give it to us. Instead . . . he leaves us peering into the gaping space of an ending that never comes.[73]

The women at the end of the original ending of Mark are cast in that space of "not yet," not yet experiencing life in light of the resurrection. They are invited into that space, a future where death does not have the last word. But instead of embracing it, they are terrified, mute, and frightened into leaving.

But this isn't the ending of the Gospel of Mark that we now have in the canon. Later interpreters of the Christian story added a more resolute, triumphant ending, where Jesus appears to Mary Magdalene and then to the male disciples, instructing them to proclaim the good news to all creation. In her assessment of how to wrestle with the different endings in Mark, Jones proposes, especially for those living in the aftermath of trauma, that it might be pastorally valuable to pause at the original ending, making more visible the ruptured character of the narrative.[74] It might help those living with serious illness and the trauma that often accompanies it to talk about how an unexpected future of more life might be both terrifying and amazing (16:8). Jesus' cry of godforsakenness and the complicated aftermath of his bodily absence in the tomb on the third day create space for those who face the indefinite loss of an uncertain future, perhaps helping them to imagine—cautiously, hesitantly—the possibility of more beyond all the loss.

Trauma, Anomie, and the Descent into Hell

The ways that those who listen carefully to experiences of trauma and those who live with serious illness seek refuge in the

Psalms, the story of Job, and in the anguished cries of the dying Christ highlight significant moments within the Christian story that make space for the irresolution that accompanies trauma as well as space for imagining how one might go on in spite of the trauma. As I become more familiar with work being done by theologians seriously engaging trauma studies, I am intrigued by the turn made toward a scene in the Christian story where irresolution is most insistent and troubling: the space in the story between crucifixion and resurrection, the day that has come to be known as Holy Saturday. It is a day that is attended to only briefly in the biblical story, a space where meaning is elusive and hope can be hard to see.

The space between the cross and resurrection is the day that Jesus lies dead in the tomb. Other than brief mentions in Matthew, in a narrative that depicts priests and Pharisees visiting Pilate and requesting the sealing and guarding of the tomb (Matt. 27:62–66), and Luke's throwaway line that the witnesses to Jesus' killing rested on the Sabbath according to the commandment (Luke 23:56), this day between cross and resurrection seems a nonevent, a "time of waiting in which nothing of significance occurs and of which there is little to be said."[75]

To envision those who lingered near Jesus' body buried in the tomb makes more visible how the death of Jesus looked from the perspective of the women and men inside the story. Theologian Alan Lewis observes that this three-part conclusion of crucifixion, burial, and resurrection would not have been experienced by those close to Jesus as the first day in a three-day happening.[76] For the women watching the crucifixion from a distance (Mark 15:40–41) and for the disciples huddled together in fear behind locked doors (John 20:19), the cross seemed to mark the end of Jesus' story.

Consciously occupying the vantage point of the second day permits the horror and anomie of Jesus' death to come more fully into view. The devastation of those who believed Jesus to be the hoped-for Messiah becomes more recognizable. That he was crucified under the title "King of the Jews" indicates that Roman rulers of the day found him guilty of sedition, of saying or doing things aimed at inciting rebellion against the authorities. The fact that the Romans killed him and that his body lay entombed meant a decisive victory for Rome. From a preresurrection vantage point, the cross is seen as a failure for Jesus and his message.[77] His authority and vision for the future seemed to be overcome by the violence of the empire. His followers were left bereft, without a leader and stripped of any confidence in that hoped-for future.

Ancient Christians frequently wrote, preached about, and depicted this space between crucifixion and resurrection in their art. In the fourth century, Bishop Rufinus, in his commentary on the Apostles' Creed, wrote that Jesus went *ad inferna* — to hell — and the phrase stuck, being added to the creed centuries later. Lewis reflects on the significance of those words:

> It is remarkable that so terse a statement, otherwise so economic with its words, should be so profuse . . . when it speaks of the interval between the cross and Easter. Christ was not only crucified but dead; not only dead but buried. And as the Creed narrates it, that burial was neither a passive laying to rest, nor a fleeting, momentary hiatus, before the activity of the third day. On the contrary, the break is significant and occupied — an active interval in which something *happens*: "he descended into hell."[78]

Because of the threat to the conventional story line that gallops toward resolution in the resurrection, many authoritative tellers of the Christian story have protested this insistent interruption of the cross-to-resurrection narrative. Some have expressed concern that the "descent into hell" language is not supported by the biblical text; others argue that saying Christ "died and was buried" is enough while still others permit "descended to the dead."[79]

This image of Christ's descent into hell, however, remains a vital component of a theology of Holy Saturday, a theological perspective that harbors important resources for those who live in the aftermath of trauma. Shelly Rambo insists that Christ's descent into hell confirms this chapter of the Christian narrative as an "an anti-love story," a story of abandonment and separation: "The Son's cry of dereliction from the cross was not a plea but an implicit declaration; the Son *is* forsaken by the Father."[80] Rambo also draws on the writings of mystical theologian Adrienne von Speyr, who says of Christ in hell, "He is in the condition of the dead, *not yet resurrected*" (emphasis mine).[81] This middle space between death and resurrection, this space of hell, allows the acute sense of forsakenness to breathe even more.

At the same time, insistence on using the language of hell often ensures that Christ's descent is understood within a strongly *moral* framework. While New Testament writers speak of hell in multiple ways, there are several significant passages where "hell" is described as the realm where the ungodly are kept in bondage until the Last Judgment (cf. 2 Pet. 2:4, 9; Jude 6; 1 Cor. 5:5).[82] One interpretive thread running through Christian theology from Cyril to Aquinas to Calvin is the strong linking of Christ's descent into the domain of evil to Christ's atoning work of defeating sin, death, and the devil.

But what exactly goes on in the life of God between Good Friday and Easter? The answer, theologian Fleming Rutledge proposes, lies more within the realm of poetry than science. Even as Rutledge resists tidy, nomic explanations of what happens in that space between crucifixion and resurrection, she also insists that tellers of the Christian story must pick up on this neglected thread of Christ's descent into hell in order to respond more adequately to the "genocidal times" in which we live. Hell is a domain where evil has become the reigning reality, and Jesus' descent into that domain complicates a compact narrative arc where the saving work of Christ is accomplished by a streamlined movement from cross to resurrection. For Rutledge, contemporary theologies that are going to speak into contemporary spaces of moral evil must acknowledge that Christ's atoning work includes his suffering for the sins of the righteous and the unrighteous alike (1 Pet. 3:18). The story of the descent into hell, then, illumines Christ's taking on the sins of even the most despicable perpetrators. This is precisely what makes the descent so hellish.

To call for and craft theologies that more forcefully address contemporary situations of genocide is a most worthy goal and one that I applaud, even as my focus in this project is on suffering that often refuses to fit neatly into a moral framework. I reference Rutledge's reflections on the descent into hell because even though she focuses primarily on instances of moral evil, she also attempts to address conditions like serious illness and natural disasters. Cancers and tsunamis, in Rutledge's telling of the story, are *impersonal* or *random* evils. The essential difference between random and moral evil, she writes, "is that whereas moral evil involves both victims and perpetrators . . . catastrophes like . . . epidemics result only in victims; there are no perpetrators."[83]

While it is important to acknowledge how situations like cancer often fall outside the category of moral evil, Rutledge's intense focus on moral evil nevertheless results in her consigning those of us who live with serious illnesses to the role of victim, a role many of us reject as too constricted to make space for the agency we still possess, a role that ultimately keeps us within a moral framework that fails to adequately capture what it's like to live with an internal threat that is not easily separated from "us." Is it possible to see the story of Christ's descent into hell as a story about Christ's occupation of not only the farthest reaches of the realm where the external threats of sin dominate but also those situations where internal threats of disease reign?

Returning to Rutledge's insistence that meditations on Christ's descent into hell should be more poetry than science, I want to suggest that poetic readings of this space between crucifixion and resurrection that move beyond questions of theodicy help us understand this part of the Christian story as one that encompasses moments that are hellish not only because of the depth of sin but also because of their intense anomic suffering. As we've seen, reflections on the Psalms, the story of Job, and Jesus' cry of abandonment open up more breathing room for the types of suffering that do not have evil perpetrators but also do not, simply, leave victims in their wake.

In envisioning Holy Saturday as a narrative space for those undone by serious illness, I want to build on the poetic rendering of the death of Christ developed by Serene Jones. In her concluding meditations on how to imagine a theology of the cross that attends to issues of trauma, Jones turns her attention toward the trauma occasioned by reproductive loss. Even though her work with trauma focuses primarily on the aftermath of violent events, here Jones's theological reflections move beyond the confines of tidy moral frameworks. She explores women's experiences of loss that just happen, where the suffering cannot be contained by any crisp analysis of cause and effect, and she then imagines how we might think theologically in, with, and through them.

Jones suggests that the image of a woman's loss of a child in utero can serve as a metaphor for what happens on the cross. She proposes that the metaphor encourages Trinitarian thinking about God as a parent who witnesses the death of God's own child. The death of God's child is "a death that happens deep within God, not outside of God but in the very heart — perhaps the womb — of God."[84] There, amid this awful space of death, hope for the future also seems to die. This heartrending depiction of Mother God's loss of her Son captures the anguish of the loss while simultaneously rejecting logical explanations for the how or why of this reign of death.

While Christians have historically blamed the fall for ushering death into the human condition, more recent tellings of the story of creation focus on how death is — and always has been — an intrinsic aspect of God's good creation, including human life. And the Son's full immersion into human life, from birth to death, means that death is also intrinsic to the life of the Trinitarian God. But the chilling reality of God's womb becoming a tomb is what allows us to move this image into the realm of Holy Saturday, where the anguish brought on by the Son's death means that the space that exists between death and life is still imagined as a hellish space.[85] The Son of God suffers in awful ways. His life is cut short. His sudden, premature death is traumatic and cause for deep grief. Even more, as Rambo has proposed, the Holy Saturday moment in the Christian story suggests that, however temporarily, the bond between God the parent and God the Son is severed. In this way, death, which remains the natural end for all of us, is also rendered the final enemy (1 Cor. 15:26).

Reflecting on this dual status of death as both a natural event and an enemy, theologian Robert Jenson proposes that "what makes death the Lord's enemy, and fearful for us is that it separates lovers. . . . Having no more being would not be evil were being not mutual."[86] The meaningless suffering of the Son on the cross separates him from the love of God the Mother, while the Son's suffering and death produces suffering deep inside the body and the heart of God. In this moment of the middle day, separation, estrangement, and death dominate.

Rendering Holy Saturday as the moment when the womb of God becomes a tomb offers those of us who live with serious illnesses another imaginative space for coming to terms with bodies and lives undone by disease. On one level, this double image of life and death reaffirms that our lives have their beginnings and endings in God. On another level, however, the image also captures the devastating experience of living with cancer when one's body-self becomes encased in death. It's not just that one must navigate a hellish terrain. It runs deeper than that, with cancer and other diseases ushering the hellish reign of death *into* the body. The body becomes the enemy. This embodied reign of death can seem inescapable. And it separates us—physically, psychically, and spiritually—from those we love. Because we are embodied selves, this reign of death also entombs our will to live and our capacity for hope.

While our own experiences of entombment by cancer and other illnesses often seem like the end of the story, the message of the Christian story is that life does not end with entombment. While God the Son descends into hell, he is not ultimately consumed by the domain of death. Instead the story moves toward Easter, which reframes Christ's descent into hell to mean "that there is no realm anywhere in the universe, including the domain of Death and the devil, where anyone can go to be cut off from the saving power of God."[87] Transposing this claim of Rutledge's onto the story of God's womb-turned-tomb suggests that when we find ourselves in the space where the womb of life resembles a tomb, God shares that space with us. And because this space is located within the life of God, it is also a space where God's intimate familiarity with both losing a hoped-for future and carrying traumatic losses deep within one's body-self intersect with our own experiences of loss.

What does more life look like for those who've been entombed? In ushering her image of God who loses her beloved Son beyond the reign of death and toward salvation, Jones is careful to explain that the image is not intended to encourage women who've lost children to imagine that excruciating experience in a redemptive light. "They are not God," Jones writes, "and even for God, the suffering itself is not the source of our redemption; the persistence of love in the midst of suffering is that redemptive source."[88] Jones imagines this God who has lost her child as embracing women who have endured miscarriage or stillbirth, rocking them gently and whispering, "I know, I know." She envisions the women being comforted by this God who, in the depths of loss, has the power to love, save, and redeem. Jones imagines that women who've lost children may be able to glimpse how such suffering might not completely consume them. They witness the love and grace of God working mysteriously in and through hellish suffering to open up the future once again.[89]

This telling of the story of Holy Saturday insists that God's womb becoming a tomb is a real and defining moment in the life of God. It also insists that the severing of relationship is real and defining. At the same time, the story testifies to these moments of death and disconnection as being held within the more expansive nature of God's communal life. As Shelly Rambo proposes in her treatment of Holy Saturday, it is vital to explore the oft-neglected role of the Spirit in what happens in the life of God in this space between death and life. The Spirit of this middle space, the "fruit of love forged through death," speaks from that hellish space to all those who live with debilitating effects of trauma.[90] Whatever comes after Holy Saturday, Rambo insists, takes as its starting point that death and life are no longer opposites.

While Spirit is the form of divine presence that's most difficult to see, feel, or touch, it is also witness to the reconfiguration
of life beyond the tomb. Even more than witness, the Spirit also
weaves the strands of divine love that emerge from the tomb as
recreation and resurrection (Rom. 1:4). Contemplating the Spirit's role as a force of renewal and regeneration can help those of
us undone by life-threatening illnesses to understand ourselves
as more than victims of our disease, for embedded in the story
of Holy Saturday is a glimpse of the horizon beyond the reign of
death. This vision is empowered by the Spirit's active presence
in the midst of death, a presence that calls us toward a life that
includes but does not remain fully defined by the tomb.

Trauma and Resolvability
in a Not-Yet-Resurrection Time

One of the most challenging issues for theologians who take
seriously stories of trauma comes from questions about the possibilities of healing, recovery, and resolution. The theologies of
Jones and Rambo, along with the meditations of Wiman, situ-
ate themselves within a theological vision where trauma's irre-
solvability resists tidy envelopment within a larger resolution.

But telling the *Christian* story with such a strong emphasis
on irresolution—even for those living with trauma and serious illness—is problematic for many other tellers and hearers
of the story. For instance, Hunsinger addresses Rambo's work
directly, concerned that Rambo's theology of the Holy Saturday leaves little space for "post-traumatic growth," suggesting
that the best anyone can do is "remain" in the wake of trauma.
"Maybe the most one can claim," Hunsinger says of Rambo's
work, "is that the Christian story tells of a 'divine remaining, the
story of love that survives . . . a cry arising from the abyss.'"[91]
Even though Rambo's turn to the Spirit's remaining is not simply a static state of survival but a way of persisting that has yet
to take shape, Hunsinger wants to go beyond Rambo's emphasis on the indeterminate character of the future and the Spirit's

ongoing work. Indeed, Hunsinger insists that with conscientious support from pastors and others who participate in the healing power of God's care, trauma "can be healed and may even become a catalyst for growth."[92]

Similar to Hunsinger, Billings wants to preserve the threat of anomie in our own stories while simultaneously keeping our eyes and hearts focused on the resolution that lies at the heart of God's story. When responding to a comment about how his book *Rejoicing in Lament* does not read like a conventional memoir, Billings admits that he is interested in "anti-memoir," that is, in telling stories about his life with cancer that do not capitulate to many contemporary approaches to memoir that place the self as the center of the universe. The point of his book and of his wrestling with questions of incurable cancer and life in Christ, Billings claims, is to reaffirm that his story is enveloped into the larger, more meaningful, and (everlastingly) life-affirming story that is God's.[93]

So even though the theological positions examined in this chapter share a common goal of making more space for the disorientation and irresolution that persist in the lives of those who struggle with trauma and its aftereffects, important differences exist in their views about the dominant orientation of the narrative. For Jones, Rambo, and Wiman, the accent is on irresolution while for Hunsinger, Billings, and Rutledge, the Christian story is ultimately one of resolution. In crafting a theology for those undone by life-threatening illness, however, I want to hold on to *both* irresolution and resolution. The four moments in the biblical narrative that have been explored in this chapter demonstrate that the Christian story is more irresolute than is commonly acknowledged by many of its tellers, and highlighting that irresolution offers breathing room for those undone by illness. But even when the biblical story gets to the chapter of resurrection, it's important to acknowledge that irresolution persists. For instance, the Gospel of Luke tells of the women who go to the tomb and find no body, only men in dazzling clothes who tell them, "'He is not here, but has risen'" (Luke 24:5). An irresolute resolution persists when disciples make their way from Jerusalem to Emmaus and are joined by the risen Christ, whom they do not recognize until he breaks bread with them. And just as the story moves toward resolution in their recognition of him as the risen Lord, he vanishes from their sight (Luke 24:28–31), leaving us once again with irresolution.

Lectionaries claim the Emmaus story as an Easter story, yet Jason Micheli insists that it could just as easily be understood as a Good Friday text.[94] To claim it as an Easter story, however, illumines the paradoxical nature of Christian claims to resurrection. The story helps us realize that it's often difficult to identify resurrection, for the experience of resurrection can be fleeting and elusive. Even as Jesus Christ lives, dies, and lives again, his presence is often experienced as an absence. In Christ's resurrection, we glimpse a foretaste of the feast to come—a time of promised resolution, when our lives return to God and participate in God's eternal communion—but for now, the space where the womb is also simultaneously a tomb remains. We live, like those who encountered the risen Christ on the road, in spaces of not-yet-resurrection, where we hope for—but are not always able to glimpse—that new age.

In response to the resurrection and in anticipation of the fulfillment of God's promises that the tomb is not the end of the story, the followers of the risen Christ became church, a communal movement where Christ's resurrection is proclaimed and the followers of the resurrected Lord commit themselves to being shaped by these stories of resurrection and regeneration, even when not-yet-resurrection realities like illness, suffering, and death seem to dominate. As these not-yet-resurrection realities persist in our present age, the church continues to be called to make room for those undone by such sufferings, even as it continues to proclaim a more expansive story of a God whose own life—and whose intention for our lives—is bigger than any of the pain, even when that pain seems totalizing. Church as a space for the undone is a space where nomos is not necessarily restored but where there's room for trauma and all that illness brings with it, as well as support for "going on," even when life with illness offers little resolution.

CHAPTER 4

⸙

CHURCH FOR
THE UNDONE

Only now that I was suffering more than I ever had in my life did I learn how Christians do not have an answer for suffering or evil. What we have, I now believe, is a community through whose compassion our faith in God is evidenced and legitimated. Our faith in the suffering love of God is intelligible, then, not through abstract answers to philosophical questions but only through the love of a community who suffer with us.

—Jason Micheli[1]

After being put through the paces of having his life undone by a diagnosis of incurable cancer, Jason Micheli witnesses to what it means to be church with and for those undone by illness: the church is a community that lives out its vocation through its incarnation of the suffering love of God, a community that refuses to let those who live through awfulness go through such awfulness alone.

The theology that undergirds this vision of the church is powerful and compelling. The apostle Paul sets forth the image of the church as the body of Christ (1 Cor. 12:12–27), with one of the most distinctive characteristics of the body being that those members deemed weakest and most lowly are actually indispensable and worthy of special honor (vv. 22–23). It's a richly organic, embodied image, where each part of the body is affected by every other part, where the suffering of just a single member of the body means that all members suffer (v. 26). When church communities live up to and into this vision of the body of Christ, they embody the suffering love of God attested to in the Christian story of Christ's death and resurrection; their care of those who are undone by the sufferings of this life confirm that suffering and death do not have the final word.

Being Called to Be with the Undone

According to Paul, it's our baptism that ushers us into participation in the body of Christ (1 Cor. 12:13). Baptism is the sacrament that has its origin not only in the command of Jesus (Matt. 28:19–20) but also in Jesus' own act of being baptized, an act that marks the beginning of his vocation as healer, forgiver of sins, and proclaimer of the reign of God. Jesus' vision of what it means to be baptized in his name signals the fundamental orientation of Christian vocation as being with and for those who suffer: "'Are you able to drink the cup that I drink, or be baptized with the baptism that I am baptized with?'" Jesus asks James and John as they tell him they want to experience the glory he experiences (Mark 10:38). Jesus' response indicates that baptism ushers his followers into the full scope of Jesus' life, death, and resurrection, of being with and for others even when it is difficult and costly.

Sixteenth-century theologian Martin Luther counseled Christians on the importance of the sacrament of baptism, stressing that it is not something that occurs just once, only to be remembered as a past event. Instead, the divine grace imparted through the sacrament persists in the here and now as well as into the future, actively renewing Christian life on a daily basis through the power of the Spirit. Riffing off of Paul's image in Galatians that all who are baptized are clothed in Christ (3:27), Luther imagines baptism as a "daily dress" for our lives. Even as the power of sin continues to be a daily reality, so too the power of baptism continues to call Christians back to putting on Christ and conforming to his life.[2]

Micheli's own journey with the suffering caused by cancer has led him to reflect more deeply on what it means to conform not only to the life of Christ but also, specifically, to his death. "'Therefore we have been buried with him by baptism into death, so that, just as Christ was raised from the dead by the glory of the Father, so we too might walk in newness of life'" (Rom. 6:4). Facing his own mortality and being opened up in new ways to the suffering of others, Micheli has come to see his walk with cancer as a form of Christian vocation: "The manner in which we're sick, the way we handle our sufferings, how we die . . . all of it are ways we live out, live up to, our baptism."[3] Living out and up to our baptism in sickness and in health, in our caring for one another, in our living in the face of death, and in our dying—this is the vocation of the body of Christ.

While this compelling vision of incarnating the suffering love of God with and for those who are ill helps us imagine what the church can and should be, we must also admit that being the church with and for the undone is often challenging, difficult, and messy. From the words of Paul to the stanzas of the creeds, we hear about the oneness of the church—one in Spirit, in baptism, and in body. In reality, however, our differences often create boundaries that challenge any claims to unity. This chapter examines what it means for the body of Christ to be a church with and for those undone by illness, especially when illness is all-too-often one of those boundary-creating differences that separate us from one another. This book as a whole seeks to illuminate the land of the ill both for those who live there as well as for those who live far away. While it is ultimately a false dichotomy to insist that all of us live either in the land of the ill or the land of the well (ignoring, for example, those in remission from illness, those living with chronic pain but otherwise functioning well, or those living with a mental illness or physical disability) from the vantage point of those who are seriously ill, there often seems to be only two places to reside. Moreover, when one lives deep within the land of the ill, the land of the well seems very far away, and the residents of Wellville are often unaware of the distance one must travel to get from one land to the other. This chapter thus explores ways to move toward unity in Spirit, baptism, and body, especially when the body contains members who are trying to live with life-threatening illness.

Are Churches Located in the Land of the Ill?

When you reside in the land of the ill, it can be challenging to visit people and places located in other lands. Outside the land of the ill, everyone seems to move at a faster pace, presume a basic state of wellness, and talk a lot about the future. While the church can rightly claim that the body of Christ is made up of members of all degrees of wellness and illness, from the perspective of someone who's seriously ill, the church often seems like a place that's best suited for the well, for it can be incredibly challenging to bring one's sick body to church. Especially when one's body is in the throes of chemotherapy or other serious treatments, it is often physically too difficult to make it to church for worship or other communal events. The pain and other physical unpleasantries from cancer and treatment often prevent those who are seriously ill from being able to attend anything other than the necessary medical appointments, especially during the worst times of the illness.

As our exploration of illness-related trauma has shown, those who live with serious illnesses also tend to experience intense psychic, emotional, and spiritual distress, not just while they're in the throes of treatment but sometimes long after treatment has ended. After she was diagnosed with a rare cancer of the appendix, pastor JoAnn Post was forced to take a leave of absence from her ministerial work at her church. But even as she was unable to carry on with her regular pastoral responsibilities, she deeply missed Sunday morning worship. She was also aware that for many who are undone by illness, grief, or other awfulness, worship can be "the hardest hour of the week because all the defenses we maintain during the week are gently toppled by song and Scripture and people who love us more than they should."[4]

Knowing how hard it might be to worship at her home congregation, Post decided to attend a worship service at a church other than her own in hopes that her vulnerable body and spirit might find it less difficult to worship in a more anonymous space. Even in a church where she was known by some rather than all, Post still became overwhelmed by the mixture of worship and embraces she received from people who knew and cared for her. She fled before the service ended. "It was too much, this love,"[5] says Post, and her sudden leave-taking from the worship service was unnerving. As a pastor, she has had a life-long enthusiasm for worship and has often been confused and a little affronted when members of the congregation who were dealing with serious sadness stayed away. Why wouldn't they seek out the body of Christ, a community committed to bearing one another's burdens, especially during the worst of times?

She admits that being undone by cancer offered an explanation: "I was suddenly and unwillingly vulnerable. . . . The familiar warmth and welcome of worship was disarming enough that I allowed the walls of imagined control to relax. And in that unguarded moment of vulnerability, the truth of my situation rushed in."[6] She was forced to confront the truth of being undone by cancer, the truth of having little control over the experience of being undone, and the truth that being vulnerable, even with those who love you dearly, can be more than we can bear.

If the church is going to be a space for those who reside deep within the land of the ill, the community needs to acknowledge that sometimes, it's just not possible for those who are really sick to be physically present in the communal gatherings of the church. Before addressing how to be with those who are too ill to be physically present within a church community, however, it is also important to reflect on how the church might be a place where the undone can be just that—undone.

In Praise of Lament

What does it mean to be a church for the undone? Most church-goers would agree that the practice of worship lies at the heart of what it means to be church. And key to worship is liturgy. As the collective practices and rituals undertaken by the people of God that unite the community to God and to one another,[7] liturgy can not only open up space for undone bodies and spirits; it can also form us as a people aware of and responsive to the vulnerability that comes from being undone.

One of the realities for those who live with trauma is the way they can become stuck because they cannot integrate the traumatic experience(s) and aftermath into their lives. The ongoing reality of post-traumatic stress interrupts and obstructs the ability to find words to capture and organize thoughts on what it means to be undone. In the concluding chapters of *The Body Keeps the Score*, Bessel van der Kolk recounts the capacity of art, music, and communal rituals and rhythms to help circumvent the challenges of finding words appropriate to articulating the trauma. Such rituals and nonverbal expressions of emotion are often able to facilitate integration—physical, psychic, emotional, and spiritual—of the suffering that remains into the lives of those who have been traumatized.[8] Recovery, as van der Kolk has witnessed time and again, is facilitated through practices that involve the body renegotiating its relationship to embodied responses to trauma.

Communal worship can therefore be an important occasion for encouraging expressions of trauma to be re-formed and for offering opportunities for body-selves to be ushered into ritual spaces where trauma might be able to become more integrated. We know that one of the things religious rituals can do is to reinforce a sense of coherence, meaning, and order in times when chaos and disorder run high.[9] Such rituals invite our body-selves into practices that can make room for expressions of trauma.

The biblical stories explored in the previous chapter testify that the cry of lament begins in the body. Job's graphic depictions of bowels in tumult, of limbs in pain, and of weeping and sleeplessness testify to the fact that pain and protest are known first, and perhaps most deeply, in the body.[10] Psalms of lament also speak metaphorically and literally to the experience of body-selves becoming undone by illness and other traumatizing events. Unfortunately, however, expressions of lament tend to be relatively rare in many contemporary forms of worship. Lectionaries have excised the rawest expressions of grief or complaint in their psalms selections. Churches that do not follow a lectionary often choose psalms of thanksgiving or particular verses of trust from lament psalms while casting aside the verses of anguish. Many contemporary hymnals overflow with songs of praise while songs of lament can be difficult to find.[11]

"Particularly since my diagnosis, I feel this [lack of lament in worship] as a stinging loss," Todd Billings writes. Participating in worship while living with advanced-stage cancer has heightened Billings's awareness of the confidence Christians tend to have in petitioning God for help in difficult times or in rejoicing over answered prayers. At the same time, he has also become keenly aware of how many in his community simply do not know how to be with others when they're undone by sorrow.[12]

Practices of lament are vital, then, not just for those who live with life-threatening illnesses but ultimately for all of us as we negotiate lives filled with joys and sorrows. We want to bring our whole selves to worship, but when our spirits and bodies grow heavy with sorrow, it can be difficult to find space in worship for conflicting emotions that often accompany anguish and grief. One of these conflicting emotions that does not seem to get much attention in liturgy, worship, or the church more broadly is anger. It's not surprising that sorrow and grief are often accompanied by a sense of anger: anger that one's life is undone, anger at the toll the suffering is taking on loved ones, and anger at losing a sense of nomos about the world and one's place in it.

Recent psychological studies indicate that anger toward God is a widespread phenomenon, particularly in the United States, despite the fact that anger toward God is often perceived to be an unacceptable emotion. Psychologist Julie Exline and her fellow researchers suggest that when persons who are angry with God are not exposed to ways to address their anger and protest toward God, they may conclude that the only reasonable response to such anger is to distance themselves from God and the people of God, even to the point of foregoing the relationship altogether.[13]

What if ample space were made in worship to foster an understanding that anger and protest toward God need not lead to the rupturing (or permanent rupturing) of that relationship? What if worship liturgies encouraged enough capacity for protest to help people imagine that anger can actually be part of a close, resilient relationship with God?[14] If anger at God can be shaped through ritual enactments of lament, it can also become possible to realize that an ongoing relationship with God is a viable option. What would it look like in Christian worship to make space—as our Jewish neighbors do—for Rachel's cries of anger and protest?

Praying the Psalms and other prayers of lament corporately during worship provides an opportunity to enact something that cannot be done when one prays alone. As Billman and Migliore propose, the embodied experience of participating in a community of believers that offer prayers of lament out loud, together, not only helps incarnate experiences of loss and grief; such incarnation can also offer strength to counter the persistent threats of disorder, chaos, and anomie. When a community embodies lament, it not only helps form individual body-selves but also a corporate body able to give voice to emotions of sadness, grief, anger, complaint, agony, and hope before God. In performing such practices, the community embodies a rebuttal to the dehumanizing effects of serious illness as well as to the sense of isolation that can be a constant partner during the worst of being sick.[15] When our sorrow and anguish are acknowledged and borne with others, we can become unstuck and able to move, as the psalmist often does, toward healing and hope.

Knowing that almost half of the prayers in the book of Psalms are dedicated to lament suggests that a community that gathers to praise and give thanks to God is also called to be a lamenting community. Knowing well the stories and practices of lament will shape those who participate in them as people prepared to lament the traumas as well as rejoice in the joys that accompany us throughout our lives.

However, as JoAnn Post confessed, even those of us who've been formed by practices of worship our entire lives find the prospect of communal worship at times too overwhelming for our undone selves. Many of us stay away, even when we're physically well enough, even when we yearn to be physically present with other members of the body of Christ. During the early days after my own diagnosis, for example, when physical and psychic pain was running high, I couldn't bear to go to church. Even as the Lenten season is dedicated to opening up space for lament, I found myself too undone to mark the beginning of the season by attending worship:

> Ash Wednesday arrived and I couldn't muster up the courage to go to church. The thought of approaching the altar so that one of our pastors could make the sign of the cross on my forehead and say, "You are dust and to dust you shall return," was more than I could handle this particular February. Two of my vertebrae had already turned to ashes and I feared the rest of me wasn't far behind. I needed no additional reminder that death was near.[16]

Receiving the imposition of ashes that marks the season of Lent is a powerful ecclesiastical embodiment of lament. To have ashes smudged on our foreheads and the words of Genesis 3:19 spoken to each of us reminds us that we are all mortal and finite. This ritual reminds us that even if the land of the ill seems like a foreign place, this won't always be the case. Even if we reside deep within the land of the ill, the ritual reaffirms what we've come to know in a visceral way: that our lives are precarious and fleeting.

It can be said that the whole season of Lent invites the body of Christ to adopt postures of lament. Beginning with Ash Wednesday and lasting through Holy Saturday, this forty-day season recalls the days Jesus spent in the desert being tempted by the devil as well as the forty years of Israel's wandering in the wilderness. The time of Lent, then, is time in the church year when members of Christ's body face and reflect on Christ's suffering and sacrifice and on the ways in which sin, suffering, and death still dominate life in the here and now. The stories of Jesus' suffering on the cross and his descent into hell—places in the Christian story spacious enough to make room for those of us undone by illness and other awfulness—make up the climactic conclusion of this season before opening the way to the Easter season.

Despite being a big fan of church and communal lament, however, as well as being convinced that the body of Christ can bear the burdens of those who are suffering like no other body I know, I just couldn't bear to go to church in those early days after the diagnosis. Physically and psychically undone, I mostly stayed away. Years of attending worship and Wednesday evening church with my husband and daughters morphed into my staying in bed while the three of them went to church.

Attending worship during the worst of my illness also proved a challenge for the rest of my family. After they'd come home from church, I would hear reports from my daughters about how their formerly even-keeled dad had, once again, cried his way through the service. For my husband, church became the only safe space where he could permit himself to come undone. His job required him to keep it together at work, and he believed he needed to keep it together at home for my sake and the sake of our children. Church became the one place where he allowed himself to experience the sorrow and grief over what cancer was doing to his wife, his marriage, and his family. "When you were diagnosed," my older daughter tells me, "I sought solace in church. It was then, more than ever, that I needed God. And being in church helped me feel closer to God." Participating in worship allowed my daughters and husband to be embraced and cared for by the community and to bring those expressions of care and concern back to me. But having one's grief (or one's father's grief) so publicly on display at times proved difficult for my daughters to endure.

Lutheran Bishop Patricia Lull borrows language from Paul's letter to the Galatians (6:2) when she talks about what bearing one another's burdens looks like in particular communities of faith. "Worshipping with the same people Sunday after Sunday," Lull writes, "[means] bearing one another's burdens isn't just a concept."[17] Bearing one another's burdens, Lull claims, is the way that we embody our relationship to one another within the body of Christ. This is the image of the church I've been raised with and readily participated in for most of my life. But residency deep within the land of the ill has forced me to recognize that sharing in the burden bearing of lives undone by serious illness or other causes for deep grief likely requires many of us to take a trip to an unfamiliar land with its uncertain terrain of illness, pain, and trauma.

Venturing to the Border of the Land of the Ill

The church is often well aware that those who are ill, or recovering from an accident, or figuring out what life looks like after the death of a loved one are not going to be physically present in church and that they are in need not just of meals and prayers but also of visits by pastors, parish nurses, and other members of the congregation. It has long been the case that members of the body of Christ show up at the hospital and the homes of those who are sick, accompany those who are in treatment when they go to appointments at the clinic, drive their children to and from lessons — and the list goes on. People of faith live out their baptism and vocation as members of the body of Christ, bearing one another's burdens and being with others in their pain.

But in my conversations with people who are seriously ill as well as those who care for and about them, I hear time and again about the gifts as well as the challenges of such burden bearing. As theologian Stanley Hauerwas observes, "It is no easy matter to be with those who are ill, especially when we cannot do much for them other than simply be present."[18] We'd like to say something comforting and hopeful, but just what that might be often eludes us. We're often unfamiliar with the landscape of Cancerland and find it difficult to navigate.

While the words we use matter, it is also the case that comfort, support, and love come in other forms as well. The cancer stories explored at the beginning of this project all testify to the struggle those who are undone by illness have in finding words that speak to and for their experiences. Educator and author Parker Palmer has written about living with severe depression, but not before admitting that he was unable to write or talk about it for many years because "the experience is so unspeakable."[19] He describes with honest frankness how challenging it was to have visitors during times when the depression was at its most severe. Most of the words spoken by his friends into that space of being undone missed the mark of comfort or support.

"One of the hardest things we must do sometimes is to be present to another person's pain without trying to 'fix' it, to simply stand respectfully at the edge of that person's mystery and misery," Palmer observes. He describes one of his friends who visited regularly but rarely spoke a word. The friend would sit down next to his bed and rub Palmer's feet, occasionally commenting on how he could sense more tension in his feet that particular day or on his sense that Palmer might be growing stronger. Palmer confesses that *those* words were words of comfort: they reassured him that even in the depths of dealing with an illness that threatened to take his life, it was still possible to be seen and acknowledged by another human being. "By standing respectfully and faithfully at the borders of another's solitude, we may mediate the love of God to a person who needs something deeper than any human being can give."[20] Palmer suggests that even when we're in close proximity to someone who's seriously ill, we ultimately can only ever stand on the edges of the landscape they inhabit. We're a guest, and the unfamiliar terrain often causes us to get lost if we venture very far in.

Hauerwas pursues further the gap that exists between those who are seriously ill and those who aren't, proposing that the problem runs deeper than a benign unfamiliarity with the terrain and landscape. No, Hauerwas claims, our difficulty with being present with the ill has to do with a deeper and more troubling issue:

> Our helplessness [when being with the ill] too often turns to hate, both toward the one in pain and ourselves, as we despise them for reminding us of our helplessness. . . . Our willingness to be ill and to ask for help as well as our willingness to be present with the ill is no special or extraordinary activity, but a form of the Christian obligation to be present to one another in and out of pain.[21]

Hauerwas's claim is unnerving. Could it be that those of us whose lives bear some degree of wellness will go so far as to experience *hatred* toward those who are seriously ill because of their helplessness and their reminder that our citizenship in the land of the well can be revoked at any point? If we're honest with ourselves, many of us no doubt will be able to recall times when we have actively avoided coming face-to-face with a friend or a loved one who was really sick. We may blame our avoidance on time constraints or on uncertainty over what to say or on some other excuse. But Hauerwas's unmasking of our excuses may well reveal our own unwillingness to be so close to the traumatic effects of illness on another's life. We can't bear it for them but perhaps also for what it says about our own tenuous hold on being well.

It can be excruciatingly difficult to be with another human being who is undone by illness, but even though we often don't know what to say, we don't always need to come bearing perfect words of comfort. It can be enough to follow the lead of Job's friends' initial action: to express grief over the suffering of your friend and simply to sit and dare to be present at the edges of the bounded space of being undone by illness. As Hauerwas says, "Our presence is our doing,"[22] and that can be enough.

The problem is that just being there isn't always enough. It is the case that a "ministry of presence" can at times be in danger of morphing into a "ministry of silence" when words of comfort are desperately needed but none are forthcoming.[23] It can be cause for despair when we are desperate for a hopeful word or a prayer that alerts God to the awfulness of our condition but all we get is a ministry of silence. There are times when we long for more than stretches of silence, more than admissions that there do not seem to be words up to the task of speaking about and to the experience of being undone.

Unfortunately there's no formula for determining when silence or a prayer or a hopeful word is most needed. How can we figure this out? One way forward (a way often not taken) is to confess our sense of uncertainty about what to say and to ask the one who is ill whether a prayer is welcome or if silence is enough. Those who are undone by illness may not always be able to respond even to this invitation, but such admission can be a helpful place to begin.

Through her years as a chaplain in an oncology ward, Reverend Jann Aldredge-Clanton has come to believe that pastoral counselors can play a valuable role for those undone by illness. Pastors, Aldredge-Clanton proposes, are called on to be both learners and guides with those who are ill—learners in the sense of bearing witness to the stories told by them and guides in the offering of prayer and biblical stories that might open up ways of relating to God amid the experience of illness.[24] Words of lament from the Psalms, Job's anguished protests toward God, Jesus' cry of godforsakenness on the cross, even Christ's descent into the depths of hell are moments in the biblical story where pastors, parish nurses, and others might begin the dance of guiding and learning about what it's like to become suddenly and utterly undone by cancer or other awfulness.

Aldredge-Clanton also notes that the process of pastoral counselors' learning from and guiding those who are seriously ill is often not a linear one. Nevertheless, sharing prayers along with stories of lament, anger, grief, disorientation, and even despair can open up expressions of loss that are integral to the stories those who are ill need to tell. As was discussed in the previous chapter, weaving the language of trauma through the biblical stories that are explored may also enable those of us who are ill to move toward a more expansive telling of our own cancer stories, thus making more space for wondering about whether and how to go on, creating room for witnessing to loss of hope, and glimpsing what going on in the face of the illness and trauma might look like.

In recounting the challenges of being with those who are ill, Aldredge-Clanton is honest about the many times she witnessed expressions of anger or guilt, feelings of abandonment or being punished by God, as well as the persistent inability of many patients to envision a future for themselves with or after cancer. Such admissions by those who are ill highlight why it is so important that a ministry of presence needs at times to be more than a ministry of silence. Reading together psalms of lament or some of Job's complaints toward God can help those who are ill imagine that anger and guilt, even feeling punished or abandoned, are experiences that reside *inside* rather than outside the life of faith. Such a claim is one that needs to be heard more often by those who are undone. They need to be assured that interrogating God with the question "Why have you forsaken me?" is, in fact, an act of faith.

For pastors and chaplains who often feel pressure to have just the right words for those who suffer and struggle with how and where God is amid the pain, acknowledging godforsakenness to be an act of faith might seem like an abdication of their pastoral role. But as the reflections on the absence of God throughout the biblical text in the previous chapter have shown, the experience of godforsakenness is neither rare nor exceptional in the life of faith. It emanates from the heart of the biblical story and the faith that grows out of it. Communicating this truth loudly, clearly, and repeatedly to those who struggle to identify God's presence in their suffering can open up new avenues for integrating moments of despair into an ongoing life of faith.

Amid the sadness, anguish, anger, and feelings of abandonment that accompany those who are undone by cancer and other illnesses, Aldredge-Clanton has also witnessed numerous instances of the rekindling of hope through the storytelling she and her patients engaged in. She found that telling one's own cancer story against the backdrop of the Christian story allowed those living with advanced-stage cancer to make new discoveries about themselves. Biblical stories of lament, illness, trauma, and ways of living with and beyond the awfulness offer frameworks for interpreting the new plotlines of their lives.

Aldredge-Clanton's insights also connect with recent research on 1) how those who live with life-threatening illnesses like cancer rely on religion and religious communities for emotional support and 2) how religious resources can provide an interpretative framework to help shape one's outlook as well as behavior.[25] In my own journey with cancer, for example, mapping my story with the story of Job has opened up new avenues for understanding an ongoing relationship with God in the midst of this life. Until recently, I wasn't much of a fan of the story of Job. That Job's suffering is cast as a test of his faithfulness is unnerving; that the righteous Job demands an answer from God and never gets one is disheartening; and that all of Job's fortunes are restored at the end can be read as simply fantastical. Before cancer, I didn't see this story as helping me interpret my life.

However, returning again to Job's story after I was diagnosed has opened up new ways of seeing it and of seeing my own story. Job's and his wife's divergent ways of dealing with the awfulness, Job's refusal to accept others' attempts at making sense of his pain, and the ways that Job is able to have an ongoing conversation with God are what stand out to me now. Retelling my own story alongside Job's encourages me to tell a realistic cancer story that does not shy away from the tough stuff; it helps me claim that even though I have no answer for the why of my own suffering, I sense God's presence with me, continuing the conversation. As Aldredge-Clanton suggests, storytelling "becomes a sacrament as Divine Presence is revealed in the midst of the struggle."[26]

Figuring out how to tell one's own story when accompanied by serious illness can help one meet the spiritual challenge of finding meaning and hope amid the waiting and uncertainty of illness. Spending time with those who are ill, listening to their stories, and offering guidance through biblical stories like the ones explored in the previous chapter—these gifts can help mitigate the suffering that remains for those who are seriously ill. Being a witness to the formation of stories about living *with*—and sometimes even *beyond*—illness can help those who are ill glimpse a horizon beyond what cancer and other illnesses so often claim.

The Potentially Porous Boundaries of the Virtual Body of Christ

Being present with those undone by illnesses like cancer has thus far presumed that members of the body of Christ will be physically present with those who are ill. But in-person, face-to-face presence is not the only way that we can be with someone who is undone by illness. In our digital age, it is possible to be virtually present as well. Before I was forced to relocate to the land of the ill, the possibility of caring for those undone by illness through virtual, digital means had never occurred to me. And if it had, I likely would have dismissed the idea as neither possible nor desirable. I would have insisted that being physically present with those who suffer is what it means to be the body of Christ with and for one another and that anything less than physical presence translates into less care, less love, and less compassion. But living with cancer for close to a decade has altered my perspectives on many things, not least of which are the ways we can be present to one another across the boundaries that separate the land of the ill from the land of the well. Years of being cared for via digital technology has converted me to the power of the *virtual body of Christ* to mediate the church's care in ways that can help mitigate the isolating and alienating effects of illness-related trauma.

Part of what makes occasions like worship one of the hardest hours of the week for those dealing with debilitating illness is the prospect of going public with our diminished selves. I don't just mean our diminished sense of self; I mean our embodied selves that appear, like Job, so altered by illness and treatment as to be almost unrecognizable. In the early days after my own diagnosis, when every radiation treatment was followed by not eating, or throwing up what I did manage to eat, I looked and felt like a diminished version of myself. Some days visitors helped take the edge off the anguish of existing in that life-in-death state, but on other days, having the drastic diminishment in my body reflected back to me in the faces of those who visited was more than my undone self could bear.

Not being able to bear the physical presence of those who care about me did not mean I didn't need support. This is when e-mails, posts on my CaringBridge site, and texts (along with flowers, cards, and other gifts in the mail) offered sustained indications that I was being cared for, prayed for, and loved. On days when I couldn't bear to see or talk to anyone other than my family, the virtual presence of those who care about me helped sustain and nourish my spirit. Moreover, one of the most surprising dimensions of the virtual body of Christ for me was how virtual communication allowed me to tell my own emerging story of becoming undone by stage-IV cancer. For months following my diagnosis, most of my attempts to put words to my life rearranged by cancer were thwarted by tears. Online, however, tears would not prevent me from completing entire sentences about what it's like to go from being able-bodied to having to depend on others in order to get out of bed or into a chair.

I've written elsewhere about my life-changing experiences with the virtual body of Christ and about how digital technology offers new and surprisingly powerful ways to tell our stories of the trauma we experienced in living with cancer.[27] My conversion to the life-changing potential of technology leads me to want to think along with others in the church about how we can use digital technology to help us get closer to the land of the ill. This doesn't mean using technology to keep ourselves at a safe distance from those who are seriously ill but, instead, using it to initiate contact with those who are ill in order to discern how one might best be present with and for them.

My experiences of being ministered to in virtual ways has helped me realize that communication through digital technology offers the church another avenue for offering care for those undone by illness, and at times this form of mediated communication helps negotiate the effects of illness-related trauma in ways that face-to-face encounters cannot. It's worth considering how this new technology can be used to welcome and involve those who are undone by illness or grief or those physically limited by age or disabilities into the life of the church even when they are not able physically to get to the church building or participate in other physical gatherings of the community.[28] That the body of Christ can live out its mission virtually means that it is possible to widen and deepen the love, compassion, and support extended to those whose suffering drives them to the edges of community.

Healing and the Body of Christ

Even as virtual connections can offer new ways of supporting those who are undone by illness, we must always be conscious of the multiple ways that being the *body* of Christ calls the church to live into its vocation of ministering to the *bodies* of those who suffer. "Christ has no body but yours. No hands, no feet on earth than yours," wrote medieval mystic Theresa of Avila.[29] And when the Gospel stories talk about Christ's embodied ministry, it is impossible to miss all the stories about healing. His hands touched those who were ill and healed them. His feet took him close to those who were suffering, and he brought healing to their broken lives.

Granted, we are not Christ, and we live in a not-yet-resurrection age, where bodies still get sick and die. But if the church is called to embody Christ's compassionate love with and for those who are ill, what role does healing play in those acts of love? Many churches offer healing services along with the practice of the laying on of hands during Sunday morning worship. This practice flows out of readings of the Gospel of Luke and the book of Acts, where Jesus' touching those he healed is expanded to his followers through the laying on of hands in its association with the gift of the Holy Spirit and baptism (cf. Acts 8:17 and 9:5–6). Moving beyond the time of Paul to the early Christian context of the book of Hebrews, the laying on of hands becomes an established ritual in connection with baptism.[30]

Even as more mainstream Christian communities incorporate such practices into their worship, it continues to be the charismatic traditions that embrace these healing traditions most enthusiastically. As Frederick Gaiser notes, given the biblical witness along with testimonies from those throughout the centuries who witness to their healing, there's a strong case to be made "that God can and does use charismatic ritual and ecstatic experience in healing. People are healed, illnesses apparently succumb, the weary find rest, and God is praised."[31]

At the same time, how Christians relate to and understand the healing power of God can be a challenging subject to negotiate with those who are ill. For instance, there are ways in which the laying on of hands and healing prayers can bring more stress than comfort. Theologian Nancy Eiesland, who lived for much of her life with serious physical disabilities, expressed deep ambivalence about how these practices are sometimes done. Eiesland's Pentecostal upbringing brought her body-self into frequent contact with the practice of healing touch, and she experienced many times an expectation by those doing the laying on of hands that she would be changed from a person with disabilities into a person who no longer had any. Failure to reach such an outcome was at times characterized as *her* failure for not wanting healing badly enough or not having enough faith.

While Eiesland endured many negative experiences of the laying on of hands, she also recounts occasions where the practice was restorative, even redemptive. After she had spent months in the hospital as a child having her body rebuilt, several elderly nuns touched and cried over her body. "From that early age," Eiesland writes, "I recall the physical sensation of having my body redeemed for God as those spiritual women laid hands on me, caressing my pain, lifting my isolation."[32] Through the gift of grace bestowed on her body-self by the nuns, Eiesland experienced her body as belonging *in* church rather than as a body that was marginalized or excluded from the body of Christ. Prayers of healing were accompanied by expressed lament over the realities of living in a not-yet-resurrection age, where bodies bear the scars of living in a limited, finite world where death remains our natural end as well as, very often, the final enemy.

While Eiesland worked to reject the insistence that her healing was dependent on the strength of her own faith, it is the case that others embrace this view as the source of their hope. One of my coffee-shop conversations a couple of years ago was with a twenty-something woman with stage-IV cancer. Moving into remission after traveling across country to receive the most intensive medical treatment possible, this woman began attending Christian healing seminars that eventually led her away from any and all medical treatment.

Even though she and I shared a common Christian faith, we had very different opinions about whether medical treatments for cancer can be considered one of the ways God works healing in the world. As we talked over coffee, I realized that my approach of relying on multiple forms of healing—from the best forms of medicine available to me for treating the disease to healing practices outside of Western medicine (such as acupuncture, yoga, and healing touch) as well as healing practices of the church— was strongly at odds with this young woman's approach. I wish I had found better words at the time to talk about healing in the context of a finite and limited world—to claim, as Todd Billings does, that prayers for healing from cancer and other diseases need to be paired with ongoing lament and expressions of deep loss.[33] Even with the promise of resurrection and new life, we continue to live in a time of not-yet-resurrection where death is still our end and healing is often of a different order than a cure.

Just as I seek out medical treatment for the cancer, my family and I also seek out the laying on of hands and healing prayers, both regular practices at the church we attend. The physical experience of hands resting on our shoulders, of being anointed with oil, and of having my health along with the health of my family prayed for have become stabilizing, nourishing rituals for all of us. They are public, physical gestures that we are in need of prayer and healing. It's also become a source of comfort to receive a public, physical embrace. All of these are public, bodily enactments of our church community's care for us as we continue to walk this journey with cancer.

Ours Is Not the Only Suffering

This side of resurrection, healing in Christ is always cruciform.[34] When practices of healing are up front about the not-yet-resurrection nature of our bodies and our power to enact healing, they can encourage those who are ill to bring their trauma and grief to church with them and to offer those burdens up for others in the community to share. Including healing prayers and the laying on of hands in worship can also make more visible how many of us are in need of healing. Many years ago, a pastor friend of mine who was staying with us ended up being in worship when our church offered healing prayers. As we watched people line up for prayers, my friend leaned over and whispered, "Look at all these lovely people in need of healing."

What a simple and profound observation: the body of Christ is made up of members in need of healing. As Gaiser suggests, the gospel calls the church to embody a vision not just of individual health but of communal well-being:

> *We* are well, not just I. Not just the observation that one's own religious faith and positive attitude are the greatest of all placebos: "Make use of this, and *you* will feel better."

But what of the other? What of the world? What of creation itself? Are they better? If those are [our] concerns, then the character of God and the content of faith will make all the difference.[35]

To be part of the body of Christ means that our own well-being is intertwined with the well-being of other members of the body. Therefore, it's never just about our own condition of relative health or illness but always about the condition of the larger "we."

In his reflection on spending so much time in clinics, hospitals, and chemo rooms with others who live with life-threatening illness and its attendant trauma, Micheli writes, "Cancer doesn't make you wonder, 'Why me, God?' . . . No, cancer throws you in the scrum and makes you ask, 'Why them, God?'" All this witnessing of other people's suffering also leads Micheli to lodge a provocative critique against the story of Job. Having to share so many small spaces with others being treated for cancer, Micheli comes to the conclusion that the cast of characters in the book of Job is too small. "Job never so much as goes to the doctor's office. Job never encounters anyone who is suffering as much as he is."[36]

Micheli's recognition of how much others are suffering is no small insight. It illustrates that the experience of being undone can, at times, open us to the vast landscape of the land of the ill and to realize how unaware we were of what this land and its inhabitants really looked like until we took up residence there ourselves. Living out and up to our baptism into Christ's death, then, can come through our own willingness to be present with others in that deeper space of a common familiarity with the landscape of suffering due to illness. Being with someone who knows the terrain can offer a rare comfort.

Even as he tries to live into this unwanted vocation of being much more aware of how much suffering there is due to illness, Micheli's telling of his own story of living with cancer is as much about how he sees his own failure to live up to his baptism as it is about how he embodies his calling to be a follower of Christ. He confesses that his experiences with cancer have led him to realize that most members of his church are "better Christians" than he believes himself to be. He recounts the story of his friend Brian, who takes Micheli to his infusion treatment only to have Micheli throw up and pass out simultaneously. Micheli writes, "He caught me from hitting the floor and then wiped the vomit from my mouth, and only semi-conscious, I apparently said to him, 'I'd never do this for you. You're a much better Christian than me.'"[37]

While residency in the land of the ill can at times elicit deeper empathy from us about the sufferings of others and a stronger willingness to be with others in times of awfulness, it doesn't always work that way. Trauma, the pernicious suffering that remains, can consume and overwhelm us to the point where the only suffering we are aware of is our own. The late cultural critic Christopher Hitchens, whose frankness was inescapable, even in his own dying from stage-IV esophageal cancer, described the challenge this way: "Cancer victimhood contains a permanent temptation to be self-centered and even solipsistic."[38] We see the illness as actor, and ourselves, as victim, robbing us of agency or responsibility toward the others who grace our lives.

Of course it's vital to affirm that those who have to negotiate the perpetual internal threat of illness certainly do need to focus on the self, likely in unprecedented ways. But the kind of self-preoccupation that's necessary for dealing with serious illness can also threaten to eclipse our ability to understand what's happening to those around us, perhaps particularly those closest to us. As discussed in chapter 2, research on family members who experience a traumatic event indirectly show that they react in ways similar to the ones who experience the trauma directly. The emotional, psychic, and spiritual suffering that accompanies diagnosis and treatment of an illness like cancer takes its toll on families as well, a reality that can sometimes get lost in the piles of suffering that surround the one who is ill.

"It's worse . . . being the spouse," a friend confided in me recently as we chatted on the sidewalk near her house. My body reacted before my words could catch up. I took a step back from this friend who had leaned into my personal space to whisper

what sounded to me like blasphemy. *"That can't be,"* I whispered back, when I couldn't hold my breath any longer. "I know," said my friend. "I never would have believed it either. But I tell you, *it's worse."*

This awful truth was being imparted by a friend who, after having come through grueling months of treatment for colon cancer, had recently been relegated to the role of "spouse of someone with cancer" when her husband was diagnosed with lung cancer weeks after she completed her treatment. Unfortunately for me, my friend qualifies as a trustworthy source, and as she proceeded to flesh out just *how* it was worse to be the spouse than to be the one with the cancer, I became aware of my lingering investment in my own suffering being the most important because it was the worst. Knowing that being the person *with the cancer in her body* was the worst position to be in was often integral to what little nomos my story of life with cancer had.

Of course, my friend's proclamation that it's worse to be the spouse than to be the one with the cancer wasn't a blanket statement meant to apply at all times, in every situation. Certainly there are times when it *is* worse to be the one with cancer, and other times (apparently) when it's worse to be the spouse. But my friend's admission helped expose for me the way in which life with cancer continues to present me with the threat of anomos. Apparently I can't even hold on to the "reassurance" that it's me whose life cancer has most undone. That reality is hard to integrate into the cancer story I've gotten really good at telling. My friend's awful endurance of cancer for herself and her spouse within the same year has worked its way into my psyche and spirit, helping me realize that I still have work to do in paying attention to and understanding the kinds of suffering that remain for my family members in the wake of nine-plus years with me and my cancer.

I find it a bit ironic that even though Christopher Hitchens was himself an atheist and serious critic of religious understandings of what it means to be human, his analysis of how human beings operate shares some important similarities with Christian diagnoses of sin. Hitchens's insight about our temptation to be consumed by our own situation when we're ill also makes visible how being formed by Christian practices of confession and the sacrament of Holy Communion are poised to place the lives of those undone by illness into a wider framework of understanding where those of us who are ill can learn that we still have agency and responsibility and are not fully defined by the place of undoneness. In addition, one of the reasons the practice of Holy Communion is a frequent one in many communities is that we need regular reminders of the way that we try to make sense of our lives by using frameworks that put ourselves at the center of the universe. These frameworks often limit our ability to live out vocations of caring for those who suffer and prevent regular opportunities to confess those limitations and be forgiven for them.

Holy Communion in a Not-Yet-Resurrection Time

In many Christian communities, the sacrament of the Lord's Supper is integral to experiences of worship. The sacrament is a visible sign of God's saving grace that frames Christians' relationships to God and to one another, calling us to admit our brokenness to ourselves, to one another, and to God, and to receive the gift of forgiveness and an opportunity to live differently in the future.

It's not surprising that the sacramental practice of Communion tends to be seen in a moral framework of sin and redemption. While I have attempted to think beyond Christianity's tight moral framing in order to make more space for the suffering that does not come from the misuse of human agency, now is the time to affirm that just because many of us who live with serious illnesses resist placing our illnesses—and our life with illness—within a tidy, moral, cause-and-effect framework does not mean that our entire existence stands outside a moral construct of sin and the need for redemption. Our embeddedness in networks of sin and injustice persists even when we're ill. As Hitchens suggests, our predisposition to serve ourselves over others remains. Even when trauma is present, we still say and do things we shouldn't. Even in a state of being undone by illness, we stand in need of forgiveness, and we are called to forgive others for the hurtful things they have said and done.

That said, the horizon of the sacrament of Communion also extends beyond a moral framework to envision a life beyond the suffering and the death where feasting at the Table becomes an eschatological reality. The Lord's Supper is a meal that remembers Christ's life, death, and resurrection, and it anticipates the time of cosmic recreation of finite, ill, good bodies. That the meal can be traced back to Jesus' Last Supper with his disciples reveals how closely the sacrament is linked to his death. At the table with his disciples, Jesus blesses the bread and shares it with them, proclaiming that it is his body and they are to eat it in remembrance of him. He blesses the cup and shares it with them, saying that it is the new covenant poured out in his blood. Because one of his disciples will hand him over to the authorities to be killed, however, the meal contains within it space for lament over the ways in which sin and death continue in this not-yet-resurrection time. Christ indicates the not-yet expression that is part of the meal when he tells them he will not partake again in this meal until the time of God's reign (Luke 22:14–23).

From the earliest days of Paul's ministry, the community's coming together around the Table to remember Christ's life and death through bread and wine has been its central sacramental act. But this meal is much more than merely a ritual of remembrance. Jesus' own words focus neither on the present nor the past; instead, they look forward to that time of eschatological feasting. As theologian Dirk Lange notes, the enactment of the Lord's Supper shifts the focus of the ritual away from death toward the question of life.[39] When we partake in this meal, we bear witness not only to the diseased, sinful, and broken character of our bodies and lives, but we also allow Christ's acts of giving thanks, blessing, breaking, giving, and sharing to take shape in our lives, anticipating a time when all lives will be fully oriented toward such living.

Celebration of the meal is the church's corporate witness to the hope that God's Spirit will renew the face of the earth, even as we know that resurrection is not yet our all-encompassing reality. Our lives still bear the marks of the sufferings not just of disease and diminishment but also of the threat of having those experiences come to define our lives and our actions. Therefore, Christ's presence in the meal, along with our enactment of it—the taking, blessing, breaking, and giving—summons our lives to open up to the horizon that's bigger than our sufferings, bigger than limited stories we are tempted to tell about our conditions. That posture of hope, however, remains embedded in this time of not-yet-resurrection where death too often seems to reign. Paul writes, "For as often as you eat this bread and drink the cup, you proclaim the Lord's death until he comes" (1 Cor. 11:26). Proclaiming his death never remains separate from proclaiming that death is not the final word, but how do we talk about hope in a not-yet-resurrection time? It is to that question we now turn.

CHAPTER 5

───────── ⬭⬭ ─────────

NOT-YET-RESURRECTION HOPE

Hope is dangerous, and yet it is the opposite of fear, for to
live is to risk.

—Rebecca Solnit[1]

As our explorations of life with cancer have shown, becoming
undone by illness and the trauma that often accompanies it presents chronic challenges to the language and practices of hope. It
becomes risky to talk about hope in the future when one's future in
this body, on this earth, may well be seriously eclipsed by disease.
But for Christians, hope is nevertheless an expectant language, a
vocabulary that indicates a trust in a God who called a good creation into being—the God who, in the person of Jesus, lived, died,
and rose to overcome death. It is a trust that this God is the author
of a future resurrection of the dead for humanity and all creation,
where evil, suffering, diminishment, and death will be vanquished
once and for all. Christian talk of hope often seems anything but
risky, for the role of the Christian is to trust in this strongly nomic
vision of life beyond death. Hope, then, becomes a confidence
directed at a future that ends in resurrection and resolution.

But having one's life undone by serious illness or other awfulness can seriously restrict one's capacity to hope. When we take seriously the trauma that those who are ill often live with, we realize that those who are really sick often stay stuck in the fear they know rather than living in hope that can help them carry on.[2] When we look at the origins of Christian vocabularies of hope, we find Paul, a man who endured persecution as well as physical ailments[3] in his role as an apostle for Christ. In addition to dealing with his own challenges, Paul spent his ministry being with and writing to those who struggled to hope and trust in God's promised future amid lives that bore all the wounds of a not-yet-resurrection time.

Therefore, Christian teachings about things like hope have often morphed into tidier, more strongly nomic frameworks than they were in originally. I thus propose returning to some of Paul's words of hope to see how they might help us form a vocabulary of hope for those undone by serious illness. In particular, I propose turning to the words Paul uses in his first letter to the church of Thessalonica, a community that was struggling to hope amid suffering and death. In his letter, Paul offers a vision that embraces both risk and trust; it's one that refuses to deny the trauma that comes with suffering and death but also one that refuses to limit hope to the terms set by this not-yet-resurrection time.

Hope Threatened by Fear

Paul talks about hope in many of his letters; but in the first letter to the church in Thessalonica, he writes to a fledgling community of faith that is having trouble figuring out what it means to hope in the face of debilitating suffering and death. As Christians, the members of the church in Thessalonica believe in the resurrection of Christ; as Christians of the first century, they also believe the return of the risen Christ is going to happen in their lifetimes. The days before Christ's return continue to accumulate, however, and some beloved members of their community die. The Thessalonian Christians are heavy with grief, struggling to figure out what it means to trust in God's promised future while their lives seemed wholly defined by a time of not-yet-resurrection.

Paul gets word of their crisis of hope and pens a letter to comfort them. He writes,

> But we do not want you to be uninformed, brothers and sisters, about those who have died, so that you may not grieve as others do who have no hope. For since we believe that Jesus died and rose again, even so, through Jesus, God will bring with him those who have died. For this we declare to you by the word of the Lord, that we who are alive, who are left until the coming of the Lord, will by no means precede those who have died. For the Lord himself, with a cry of command, with the archangel's call and with the sound of God's trumpet, will descend from heaven, and the dead in Christ will rise first. Then we who are alive, who are left, will be caught up in the clouds together with them to meet the Lord in the air; and so we will be with the Lord forever. Therefore encourage one another with these words.
>
> (1 Thess. 4:13–18).

For those of us in the twenty-first century, Paul's words may well seem to be strange words of comfort. They describe a cosmic scene of Christ descending from heaven to oversee the resurrection of the dead and of those who are still alive being caught up in the clouds to meet Christ in the air. This scene has inspired modern-day visions of the rapture—a nomic vision of a predicted end of time when all Christians, living and dead, will be raised to be with Christ. Christians who talk about Paul's words in First Thessalonians tend to be ones who want to talk about the end of the world.

"People have always been good at imagining the end of the world," writes cultural historian Rebecca Solnit.[4] What we humans are not so good at, Solnit observes, is cultivating hope when the future seems unsettled and uncertain. Solnit directs her words toward those of us who often grow weary over how little progress toward justice can often be detected despite our best efforts; she offers instead a vision of "hope in the dark," one that relies on an alternative to the logic of a future of *either* victory *or* defeat. "To be hopeful is to take on a different persona," Solnit says. It's risky, taking on a persona of hope, since it's "ultimately a form of trust, trust in the unknown and the possible."[5]

For Solnit, hope is cultivated in no small measure by the stories we tell about ourselves. She notes that we often present the stories of history in terms of either winning or losing, and this tidy framing can limit our views of what's possible in the present as well as the future. In order to take on a persona of hope, Solnit insists on moving beyond a moral framework of winners and losers to a *trust* in the possibilities of what might yet come to be. At the same time, Solnit suggests, hope is not simply focused on the future; rather hope gets practiced and lived out, with others, in the here and now.[6]

One of the key differences between Solnit's vision of hope and a Christian vision of hope like the one Paul offers to the Thessalonians is that Paul's attention is directed not just toward what might happen tomorrow or next week but also toward what lies beyond this life. While any Christian vision of hope should not shy away from talking about death and what might lie beyond, it's also important to notice that the vision of hope from Paul's letter to the Thessalonians begins with the experience of this world, of being undone by grief and with confronting what it means to *live* in the face of death. Paul offers a vision of hope aimed at comforting those who are grieving. The persons he's addressing are not necessarily undone by *illness* but are grieving the suffering that *just is*.[7] Friends and loved ones are dying, and they wish it weren't so. The Thessalonians are also fearful and anxious about what the future holds for those who have died. Paul offers them a vision of hope for this time between death and resurrection—a kind of Holy Saturday for those who wait for the coming of the Lord.

A Hope Spacious Enough for Grief

Paul's admonition to the Thessalonians, that they not grieve as others do who have no hope (v. 13), has proven to be a difficult passage for Christian interpreters, particularly for those who are wedded to strongly nomic versions of the death-to-resurrection narrative. While biblical scholars consistently point out that Paul is *not* saying that Christian hope cancels out the need to grieve,[8] tellers of the Christian story at times embrace a different interpretation of this passage: that having hope in life beyond this one means foregoing the sorrow, grief, and lament over losses like those that accompany life with serious illness.

I recently heard firsthand how misapplications of this line from Paul continue to have a place in Christian talk about hope. I spoke at a local church and used this passage as a way in to thinking about trauma, illness, and hope. Afterwards a woman sought me out and told me that in the days following her daughter's death by cancer in her early twenties, some friends wanted to make sure she understood that because she believed in the resurrection, there was no need to grieve her daughter's death. The harm inflicted by this vision of hope was palpable. This anguished mother believed in her gut that they were wrong, that her love for her daughter could not be expressed in any way other than deep sorrow for the loss of her young life. To believe in a future resurrection did not negate the compulsive need to grieve the many layers of losses that a premature death to cancer forced into her life.

Rather than recommending that we skip the grieving, Paul proposes that having hope in the resurrection *shapes* the way we grieve in this time before resurrection. His proposal is likely offered as a contrast to other views of death prominent in his day, views common in our day as well. Greco-Roman views of the time held that nothing lies beyond death. One Latin tomb inscription communicates this sentiment well: "I was not; I was; I am not; I care not."[9] As the Thessalonian community faces the eclipse of more life on earth for those beloved to them, Paul offers a different vision: that because of Christ's life, death, and resurrection, our lives and our vision of hope look different than they would if we believed this life is all there is.

Even when we orient our lives toward a future with God, there still should be space for grief in the here and now over the suffering that simply is. Recall that studies of illness-related trauma reveal that life in the throes of serious illness often robs us of our ability to imagine a future this side of resurrection. In the throes of being undone by cancer, the goals we have for our future selves are put on hold; they hang in the balance, suspended by uncertainty.

According to cancer chaplain Jann Aldredge-Clanton, the goals we set for our lives are "the plot elements that help give structure to [our] life stories."[10] She thinks this is why many of us who live with cancer and serious illnesses press our oncologists for statistics regarding life expectancy for people who have what we have. Paul Kalanithi admits that even though in his role as a physician he'd been coached to avoid offering statistics, one of the first things he asks his own oncologist about is what the statistics said about his condition.[11] When my daughter was in the process of choosing whether to attend a college farther away or closer to home, she wished for statistics that would indicate how long her mother was likely to live. We are invested in data that helps reinforce some sort of confidence in what the future has in store for us.

A common sentiment of those who've come through the other side of diagnosis and treatment for cancer is that they wish they had known they were going to live beyond the cancer.[12] Many of us who've lived with cancer are faced with negotiating more days of life after struggling to accept that our days on earth might be very few. Some of us, however, won't live beyond the cancer, and none of us will live beyond every illness that comes our way. While much of this book has been focused on the *how of living* with the cancer and the trauma that often accompanies it, framing a discussion of hope with Paul's words to the Thessalonian Christians suggests that hope also talks about the *how of dying* amid the cancer and its attendant trauma. While Christian hope often includes talk of healing, Frederick Gaiser reminds us that all those who experienced healing within the stories of the Bible still die, eventually. Healing in Christ in this time of not-yet-resurrection is ultimately always cruciform.[13]

As discussed earlier, many obituaries that talk about death from cancer are often framed in military imagery. They state that the person "lost the battle" to cancer. A friend of mine expressed his frustration with this approach in a way I hadn't considered. When described with military imagery, he protested, "the last act of this person's life is one of failure."[14] The one who is ill loses the battle by dying.

What might it look like to frame one's death due to illness in a way that holds hope and grief together rather than using a framework of winning and losing? A recent obituary for a woman in my community, Leslie Nelson Tengwall, carves out a different path than the morally tinged win-or-lose approach, one that makes space not just for the awfulness of cancer but also for the more that our lives always are. The obituary opens by saying that Tengwall ended "an eleven-year journey through the muck that is cancer." It also acknowledges the ways in which cancer diminished Tengwall's ability in what she could do, but the writers of the obituary refused to let cancer have the last word on her life: "To the very end, Leslie taught us what it means to live and die with grace and courage."[15]

While hoping to live beyond the cancer is a primary hope of those living with the disease, Aldredge-Clanton bears witness to other forms that hope can and does take for those whose illness leads toward the threshold of death. She recounts how those living near death have hoped for changes in relationships, for a life with manageable pain, for experiences of spiritual growth, for life with God beyond their earthly life.[16] Rather than giving up on hope, they are rewriting their stories and their hopes for the future, facing their remaining days with grace and courage, even when life is mired in the muck that is cancer.

Several years ago, I talked with a group of parish nurses about how to address these issues with those who are dying. One nurse shared with the group her approach. When she is with some-one facing death, she often opens the conversation by asking,

"What are you thinking about most these days?" Rather than predetermining the parameters of the conversation about what they are facing, this nurse gently lays a question before those who are near death and invites them to venture into that holy and potentially unsettling place of what is most pressing to them at this moment. In his letter to the Thessalonian church, Paul calls on its members to surround one another amid their anxiety and grief and to encourage one another with words of hope—hope that there's more than the finality of death they've recently experienced in their community, more than the suffering they're forced to endure. Paul implores the church not only to talk of the hope Christians have to experience the grace and joy of life in the here and now but also to be encouraged that this life, with all its sadness, brokenness, joy, and beauty, is not all there is.

Imagining Resurrection While Living in a Not-Yet-Resurrection Time

In 1 Thessalonians 4, Paul talks about the dead being raised with Christ, a claim of bodily resurrection that Christians across the world continue to confess almost two millennia later. Yet many of us likely wonder what this can possibly mean in a world in which we know well the science of decomposing flesh and in which cremation is growing in popularity. After the tragic death of his son in a mountain climbing accident, theologian Nicholas Wolterstorff spent significant time wondering what the eschaton will be like. He writes,

> I wonder how it will all go when God raises [Erik] and the rest of us from the dead? . . . [There will be] so many, so innumerably many. I see them stretching way back, their faces eventually becoming just a brownish haze from here. Everybody is known by somebody in that crowd, but the memories usually trail off somewhere so that up front here we know only a very few. God alone has them all in mind.

I don't see how God's going to bring it all off. But I suppose if he can create he can re-create. I wonder if it's all true? I wonder if he's really going to do it?[17]

For Wolterstorff, Christian hope is a posture that strives to trust that the God who creates is also the God who re-creates—that this God is the One who will really bring life out of death.

While folks like Wolterstorff are honest in their wonderings about how the resurrection of the dead will actually work, many others have turned to Paul's words of comfort to the Thessalonians for confirmation of a literal description of what re-creation will look like. First Thessalonians 4:15 describes the *parousia* or "coming" of the Lord. A term used in the ancient world to describe the arrival or visit of a king or emperor, "the Parousia" has come to refer in theological parlance to the second coming of Christ. Even as the Thessalonians passage has proven fertile ground for those thinking about a rapture that precipitates the end of the world, many theologians and biblical scholars caution against a literal reading of this passage. As Daniel Migliore suggests, the language of Christian hope "is language stretched to the limits."[18] It's language rich in symbolism and imagery; it does not form the basis of a tidy nomic vision of the future but instead opens up ways of imagining how hope in the Parousia might shape our living in this not-yet-resurrection time.

If we approach Paul's vocabulary of hope imagistically rather than literally, what might a reading of the Parousia depicted in 1 Thessalonians 4 tell us about the kind of hope that encourages those who are undone by grief brought on by suffering and death, and in particular, the suffering brought on by life-threatening illness? One way to read this passage, biblical scholar Laura Nasrallah suggests, involves paying attention to the "spatiality and politics" of Paul's words. Imagining what this scene would look like spatially, Nasrallah points out that the dead were buried in cemeteries outside the city walls. If they were to rise and be the first to greet Christ, it would mean that the living would join later when the procession made its way inside the city walls. Paul's vision of the Parousia in 1 Thessalonians 4, then, stands in stark contrast to expected parameters of behavior regarding how rulers were met outside the city walls by the wealthy and prominent citizens and then escorted into the city. The scene from Thessalonians features some "not-so-prominent Thessalonians who greet a different Lord."[19] It's a scene of re-creation not just of those undone by suffering and death but of social relationships and of the community's relationship with a very different kind of imperial ruler.

That the Lord's descent from heaven to earth is accompanied by a "cry of command," an "archangel's call," and the sound of a trumpet (1 Thess. 4:16) hearkens back to Jewish apocalyptic imagery found in Isaiah 27:3 and Joel 2:1. This imagery of fanfare heralding a final battle and time of judgment in the apocalyptic passages gets cast somewhat differently in 1 Thessalonians 4. While 1 Thessalonians 5 contains stronger military and moralistic imagery, the language in chapter 4 that talks of the Parousia remains broader, more spacious. The trumpet heralds movement by those who've been undone by death, movement that links them to Christ, the One who was betrayed, forsaken, and undone by suffering but also the One who traveled through the depths of hell to live again.

Building on the ways the eschatological, imperial procession depicted in 1 Thessalonians differs from conventional processions in the ancient world, biblical scholar Florence Gillman imagines how an artist might sketch the scene. Gillman suggests that if the first wave of people, the dead, were portrayed as they were when they died, the procession would undoubtedly include a large proportion of people whose lives had been tragically cut short. While some no doubt lived full adult lives, "far, far more numerous would have been the people who had died as infants, as small children, as women in childbirth, as impoverished, malnourished non-elites, and as maltreated slaves."[20] The procession imagined in 1 Thessalonians 4 speaks to the "fragility, pain, indignities, and inequities" of the lives and bodies of the ancient Thessalonians. It's a procession that includes those undone by moral failings and by individual and corporate sin and injustice; at the same time, this vision of the procession also includes space for those undone by illness and other suffering that falls outside a tidy sin-redemption framework.

A question that arises from this reading of the coming of the resurrected Christ has to do with the conditions of the bodies that will be processing from outside the city limits to inside the city walls. The image of the dead appearing as they did when they died is a powerful one, but will they remain undone, even when they arrive inside the city?

Returning to the image of the imperial procession in Paul's letter to the Thessalonians and the dead being raised and making their way into the city, we note that there are other places in the biblical story where city imagery is employed to depict what resurrected life with God might be like. One of the final scenes of the book of Revelation envisions a new heaven, a new earth, and a new city where God will dwell with members of God's beloved creation; they will be God's people, and God will be with them. In this new city God will wipe away any tears that might remain. Death will be no more, and there will be no more mourning or crying or pain (Rev. 21:1–4).

I love that vision of the re-created city. At the same time, I'm aware that Paul's vision of the Parousia in 1 Thessalonians doesn't end in the city. The image Paul offers the Thessalonian church concludes with the image of the dead and the living being taken up into the clouds to meet Christ in the air in order to be with the Lord forever (1 Thess. 4:17). As language is once again stretched to its limits, we are left wondering what kind of resurrected body we might have.

The biblical vision of re-creation is one where God makes all things new (Rev. 21:5). But what exactly might this mean for our diseased bodies? Tellers of the Christian story have consistently rejected attempts to envision life with God in fully spiritual, disembodied terms. Just what bodies might look like in this new city, however, remains a mystery. Theologians like Martin Luther suggest that just as all of us in utero know nothing about life outside the womb, so too are we in this life scarcely able to imagine what lies ahead in life with God beyond this one.[21] For Luther, faith is at heart a trust that the promises of God—like the promise of union with Christ that Paul articulates in his letter to the Thessalonians — are true. But Luther's anguished confession at the death of his beloved daughter Magdalene at age thirteen reveals that trusting in the more does not cancel out the grief: "The separation [from his daughter] troubles me beyond measure. . . . It's strange to know that she is surely at peace and she is well off there, very well off, and yet to grieve so much!"[22]

We could end here, keenly aware of our limits over what we can say and imagine, realizing that on this side of resurrection our hope will always be tinged with grief. But if we look at the biblical treatment of resurrection, there seems to be more we can say. When we look again at the resurrection of Christ's body, we realize that it was not simply a resuscitation of his earthly body, for the Gospels repeatedly testify to how those closest to Christ in life before his crucifixion could not immediately recognize his resurrected body. In his letter to the Corinthians, Paul describes the resurrected body as a spiritual body, imperishable and from heaven (1 Cor. 15:42–49).

The resurrected body is therefore different from the body we have now, but it remains a body, one made to be in communion with God.[23] While our resurrected bodies are not simply our earthly bodies resuscitated, theologian David Jenson points out that if we look to Christ's resurrection for signs of what our own resurrection might be like, we also see that something about Christ's individuality was preserved in resurrection, for eventually those who knew and loved him were able to recognize him in his resurrected state.[24]

Part of that continuity between the pre- and postresurrection Christ is the way his resurrected body continues to bear the wounds of crucifixion. These wounds suggest that resurrection doesn't erase the scars that we accumulate during our lives. But even when we march in that procession with our missing body parts and broken bones that never fully healed, Revelation's image of the New Jerusalem suggests that our wounds will no longer cause suffering.

To claim with Paul, then, that Christ will come again is more than simply saying yes to the claim that he will descend from the heavens at some future point. To encourage one another with these words means embracing the hope that while this life requires much room to grieve our losses, traumas, and sorrows, the future envisioned by the Parousia can be glimpsed and experienced in the here and now. If the second coming recalls the first, Jenson notes, "we should also expect Christ to appear in unexpected and neglected spaces."[25]

One such unexpected place might be right in the middle of a life undone by illness. While living with cancer has robbed me of much, I cannot ignore the glimpses of resurrection and eschatological feasting that have made their way right into the middle of the awfulness. One of the most enduring images for me came at a party thrown by friends of ours who had made my family and me a quilt that could serve as a tangible reminder of their love and care for us during the dark days of living with cancer. The quilting party, overflowing with people from all corners of our lives, was a celebration unlike any I'd ever attended. It was simply overwhelming to be surrounded by the joy and love shown to us by so many.

At the end of the day, it struck me that in addition to being the party of a lifetime, the quilting party had also offered me a glimpse of what the eschatological feast might be like. No other image does justice to its sacred, joyous quality. If the banquet that awaits us is anything like the quilting bee, I realized that getting sick and dying no longer seemed quite as foreboding as they had before the party. I also realized that in addition to being reassured about what's up ahead, beyond death, I was also offered reassurance about this cancerous life: that a taste of resurrection was actually possible right here, right now. This opportunity for feasting hadn't occurred back in life before cancer but right in the middle of my fractured, grief-filled life.

Due to advances in medical technology, it's becoming more possible to live long(er) and even well with incurable cancer and other life-threatening illnesses. Thus more and more of us will be trying to figure out how to talk about hope grounded in God's promises for life beyond this world that also makes its presence known in this not-yet-resurrection life, where illness and disease abide. Friend and fellow metastatic-breast-cancer traveler Camille Scheel found a way to talk about her hope in God's promised future amid the trials of cancer. Here's what she said:

> As an Episcopalian, I bow to the cross as it passes, which makes me imagine what it will be like the first time I experience the Lord in heaven; I imagine needing to bow and cover my eyes to the light. It's wonderful to think of a place that is all love, light, and peace. Feasting on the sensual nature of this world now makes me feel as if I'm choosing between two delicious meals and I can't decide which is better. That being said, I won't give up this world easily.[26]

Camille did not give up on this world easily. She lived ten long years with the disease, dying just days before I write this. Never one to shy away from the grief and the trauma that cancer continued to force into her life, she inspired many of us with her commitment to be unflinchingly honest about the awfulness while refusing to let go of the more promised to us by God.

Encourage One Another with These Words

"Encourage one another with these words" (1 Thess. 4:18). Paul's vocabulary of hope in 1 Thessalonians does not give us a blueprint for what the Parousia will look like, feel like, smell like, or taste like. But it does offer a vision of hope for resurrection for all of us whose lives and bodies bear the limitations of this not-yet-resurrection time. Even when our lives are limited by illness and the trauma and isolation that can accompany it, the promise of the Parousia assures us now that we are created not only for relationship with God and others in the here and now but for relationship with God and others in life beyond this one. We are promised that the love that binds us to God and to one another is a love that persists, even in the face of death.

The vocabulary of hope offered by Paul to the Thessalonians opens up avenues for talking about hope in ways that leave space for the ambiguity and the indefinite loss that is integral to living with life-threatening illness. Although the image of our promised resurrection does not offer resolution to our often-anomic situation, the image of a promised life with others and with Christ helps us to reframe the power of the trauma, suffering, diminishment, and death. This image of hope helps us envision that being entombed by disease is not the end of the story of our embodied lives. Our stories of lives dominated by loss of health are encompassed by a larger story of hope in the more of life, both in this world and in the beyond. The trumpets that greet the procession of diseased bodies as they move out of the tomb and back into the city signal the possibility of rediscovering a rhythm within our bodies once again.[27] Even in our still-broken bodies, we can process in the path of Christ, who beckons us to live again.

NOTES

Introduction

1. Deanna A. Thompson, *Hoping for More: Having Cancer, Talking Faith, and Accepting Grace* (Eugene, OR: Cascade Books, 2012), 142.

2. Peter L. Berger says, "Seen in the perspective of society, every nomos is an area of meaning carved out of a vast mass of meaninglessness, a small clearing of lucidity in a formless, dark, always ominous jungle" (*The Sacred Canopy: Elements of a Sociological Theory of Religion* [New York: Anchor Books, 1969], 23).

3. I'm relying again on Peter Berger's discussion of "anomy" that threatens our sense of nomos: "The sacred cosmos, which transcends and includes man in its ordering of reality, thus provides man's ultimate shield against the terror of anomy" (ibid., 27). I prefer the more contemporary spelling of "anomie" used by sociologists and psychologists. See, for instance, E. L. Maher, "Anomic Aspects in the Recovery of Cancer" (*Social Scientific Medicine* 16, no. 8 (1982): 907–12), which describes the anomie of individuals recovering from cancer who experience disorientation and threats to meaning making during their recovery.

4. Pauline Boss, *Ambiguous Loss: Learning to Live with Unresolved Grief* (Cambridge, MA: Harvard University Press, 1999), 140.

5. Shelly Rambo's definition of trauma (*Spirit and Trauma: A Theology of Remaining* [Louisville, KY: Westminster John Knox Press, 2010], 15).

6. By "trauma studies" I am referring to a field that traces its origins back to the late nineteenth-century neurological studies conducted by French psychiatrists like Jean-Martin Charcot and his most famous student, Sigmund Freud. With the insertion of post-traumatic stress disorder (PTSD) into the *Diagnostic and Statistical Manual of Mental Disorders* (*DSM-III*) (3rd ed. [Washington, D.C.: American Psychiatric Association, 1980]), the phenomenon of

"overwhelming" experience that causes a long-lasting psychic wound is studied not just by psychiatrists but in a variety of disciplines interested in exploring the aftereffects of such overwhelming experiences.

7. *Diagnostic and Statistical Manual of Mental Disorders* (*DSM-IV*), 4th ed., rev. text (Washington, D.C.: American Psychiatric Association, 2000), 467–68.

8. See the description of traumatic experiences as having "a beginning, middle, and end" in Bessel van der Kolk, *The Body Keeps the Score: Brain, Mind, and Body in the Healing of Trauma* (New York: Viking Books, 2014), 16.

9. Meredith Y. Smith, et al., "Post-traumatic Stress Disorder in Patients: A Review," *Psycho-Oncology* 8, no. 6 (Nov.–Dec. 1999): 521–37. It is also important to note that trauma theorists like Judith Lewis Herman, whose work pays close attention to situations of domestic violence, also note that van der Kolk's "beginning, middle, and end" version of traumatic events (*The Body Keeps the Score*, 16) fails to capture the recurring nature of an abusive relationship. Herman advocates for a vocabulary that more accurately captures this reality and proposes the phrase "complex post-traumatic stress disorder." See Herman's *Trauma and Recovery: The Aftermath of Violence —from Domestic Abuse to Political Terror* (New York: Basic Books, 1997), 119.

10. Nancy Jo Bush, "Post-Traumatic Stress Disorder Related to the Cancer Experience," *Oncology Nursing Forum* 36, no. 4 (2009): 395–400.

11. In the *DSM-5*, the following statement was added regarding PTSD diagnosis and serious illness: "A life-threatening illness or debilitating medical condition is not necessarily considered a traumatic event" (*Diagnostic and Statistical Manual of Mental Disorders*, 5th ed. [Washington, D.C., American Psychiatric Association, 2013], 274.) Still, there is a growing body of medical research that explores how symptoms of PTSD are present in a sizable minority of those who live with cancer. See, for example, "Cancer-Related Post-traumatic Stress (PDQ®)–Health Professional Version," National Cancer Institute , accessed January 24, 2017, http://www.cancer.gov/cancertopics/pdq/supportivecare/post-traumatic-stress/HealthProfessional/page3.

12. A precise definition of cancer-related PTSD is difficult to find. Many studies reference the *DSM-5*'s definition of PTSD (see note 11). At the same time, *cancer-related* PTSD seems to have its own distinctive manifestations, as discussed above. One the best treatments of this issue that I have found is Lindsay N. French-Rosas, M.D., Jennifer Moye, Ph.D., and Aanand D. Naik, M.D., "Improving the Recognition and Treatment of Cancer-Related Posttraumatic Stress Disorder," *Journal of Psychiatric Practice* 17, no. 4 (July 2011): 2.

13. Ibid., 3.

14. Ibid.

15. M. A. Andrykowski, et al., "Stability and Change in Posttraumatic Stress Disorder Symptoms following Breast Cancer Treatment: A 1-Year Follow-up," *Psycho-Oncology* 9 (2000): 69–78; and A. B. Kornblith, J. E. Herndon, R. B. Weiss, et al., "Long-term Adjustment of Survivors to Early-stage Breast Carcinoma, 20 Years after Adjuvant Chemotherapy," *Cancer* 98 (2003): 6679–89, as cited in French-Rosas, et al., "Improving the Recognition," 3.

16. Mary Vachon reports that only one in ten get psychiatric help. See Mary Vachon, "Psychosocial Distress and Coping after Cancer Treatment: How Clinicians Can Assess Distress and Which Interventions Are Appropriate—What We Know and What We Don't," *American Journal of Cancer Nursing* 3 (2006): 26–31; cited in French-Rosas, et al., "Improving the Recognition," 4.

17. World Health Organization, "Global Cancer Rates Could Increase by 50% to 15 Million by 2020," accessed 28 August 2017, http://www.who.int /mediacentre/news/releases/2003/pr27/en/.

18. John Green, *The Fault in Our Stars* (New York: Dutton Books, 2012), 216.

19. Rodney is one of the subjects in Rebecca Eileen Olson's, "Managing Hope, Denial or Temporal Anomie? Informal Cancer Carers' Accounts of Spouses' Cancer Diagnoses," *Social Science & Medicine* 73 (2011): 907.

20. Arthur Frank, *The Wounded Storyteller: Body, Illness, and Ethics* (Chicago: University of Chicago Press, 1997), 25.

Chapter 1: Undone by Cancer

1. Paul Kalanithi, *When Breath Becomes Air* (New York: Random House, 2016), 215.

2. Atul Gewande, *Being Mortal: Illness, Medicine, and What Matters in the End* (New York: Picador Books, 2015), 5.

3. Arthur Frank, *The Wounded Storyteller: Body, Illness, and Ethics* (Chicago: University of Chicago Press, 1997), xii.

4. Ibid., 2.

5. Arthur Frank, *Letting Stories Breathe: A Socio-Narratology* (Chicago: University of Chicago Press, 2010), 4.

6. Kalanithi, *When Breath Becomes Air,* 147–48.

7. Ibid., 149.

8. Susan Gubar, *Memoir of a Debulked Woman: Ending Ovarian Cancer* (New York: W. W. Norton & Co., 2012), 155.

9. "Statistics," Ovarian Cancer Research Fund Alliance, accessed December 21, 2016, https://ocrfa.org/patients/about-ovarian-cancer/statistics/.

10. Arthur Frank, *At the Will of the Body: Reflections on Illness* (Boston: Houghton Mifflin, 1991), 13.

11. Gubar, *Memoir*, 154.

12. Carrie Host, *Between Me and the River: A Memoir* (New York: Harlequin, 2011), 189.

13. Ibid., 11.

14. Audre Lorde, *The Cancer Journals* (San Francisco: Aunt Lute Books, 1980), 24.

15. Ibid., 27.

16. Ibid., 47.

17. Gubar, *Memoir*, 74.

18. Ibid., 245.

19. Ibid., 248.

20. Ibid., 262.

21. Susan Gubar, *Reading and Writing Cancer: How Words Heal* (New York: W. W. Norton & Co., 2016).

22. Barbara Ehrenreich, *Bright-sided: How Positive Thinking Is Undermining America* (New York: Picador Books, 2010), 26.

23. "How Common Is Breast Cancer?" American Cancer Society, last revised January 4, 2018, http://www.cancer.org/cancer/breastcancer/detailed guide/breast-cancer-key-statistics.

24. Kate Bowler, "Death, Prosperity Gospel, and Me," *New York Times*, February 13, 2016, accessed February 13, 2017, https://www.nytimes.com /2016/02/14/opinion/sunday/death-the-prosperity-gospel-and-me.html.

25. Ehrenreich, *Bright-sided*, 32.

26. Ibid.

27. Gina Kolata, "In Long Drive to Cure Cancer, Advances Have Been Elusive," *New York Times*, April 24, 2009, as quoted in Ehrenreich, *Bright-sided*, 27.

28. Ehrenreich, *Bright-sided*, 196.

29. "A Positive Attitude Does Not Help Cancer Outcome, *Medical News Today*, February 9, 2004, http://www.medicalnewstoday.com/medicalnews .php?newsid=5780, as quoted in Ehrenreich, 42.

30. Ehrenreich, *Bright-sided*, 42.

31. Ibid., 26.

32. A helpful article exploring multiple sides of this debate is Sharon Begley, "Most Cancer Cases Arise from 'Bad Luck,'" *Scientific American,* March 24, 2017, accessed March 30, 2017, https://www.scientificamerican.com /article/most-cancer-cases-arise-from-bad-luck/.

33. Susan Gubar, "Living with Cancer: Coming to Terms," *New York Times* blog post, January 22, 2015, accessed March 31, 2017, http://well.blogs .nytimes.com/2015/01/22/living-with-cancer-coming-to-terms/?_r=0.

34. J. Todd Billings, *Rejoicing in Lament: Wrestling with Incurable Cancer and Life in Christ* (Grand Rapids: Baker Books, 2015), 151.

35. Ibid., 18.

36. Ibid., 2.

37. Deanna A. Thompson, *Hoping for More: Having Cancer, Talking Faith, and Accepting Grace* (Eugene, OR: Cascade Books, 2012), 52.

38. Billings, *Rejoicing in Lament*, 56.

39. Ibid., 116.

40. Ibid., 10–11.

41. Ibid., 101.

42. Ibid., 89–90.

43. Ibid., 150.

44. Ibid., 151.

45. Host, *Between Me and the River*, 59.

46. Billings, *Rejoicing in Lament*, 85.

47. John Thompson, "An Exhortation to Martyrdom," (Pasadena, CA: Fuller Theological Seminary, 1997), 3, as quoted in Billings, *Rejoicing in Lament*, 109.

48. Todd Billings, speaking in "A Poet and a Theologian Discuss Incurable Cancer—Christian Wiman and Todd Billings," Western Theological Seminary's James I. Cook Endowment in Christianity & Literature and the Osterhaven Lecture Series, March 31, 2015, accessed February 20, 2017, http://jtoddbillings.com/2015/03/penetratingly-honest-and-expansively-hopeful/.

49. Christian Wiman, *My Bright Abyss: Meditations of a Modern Believer* (New York: Farrar, Straus & Giroux, 2013), 177.

50. Christian Wiman, "Love Bade Me Welcome," in *Reckonings: A Journal of Justice, Hope, and History,* accessed February 10, 2017, http://www.reckonings.net/reckonings/2013/10/love-bade-me-welcome-by-christian-wiman.html.

51. Wiman, *Bright Abyss*, 56.

52. Ibid., 148.

53. Ibid., 72.

54. Ibid., 75.

55. T. S. Eliot, "The Dry Salvages," in *Four Quartets* (New York: Harcourt, 1971), 38.

56. Wiman, 157.

57. Ibid., 155.

58. Ibid., 17.

59. Ibid., 69.

60. Ibid., 178.

61. Judith Butler, *Precarious Life: The Powers of Mourning and Violence* (New York: Verso Books, 2006), 23.

62. Cathy Caruth, "Preface," in *Trauma: Explorations in Memory* (Baltimore: Johns Hopkins University Press, 1995), as quoted in Shelly Rambo, *Spirit and Trauma: A Theology of Remaining* (Louisville, KY: Westminster John Knox Press, 2010), 3, footnote 2.

Chapter 2: Living with Trauma Brought on by Illness

1. Shelly Rambo, *Spirit and Trauma: A Theology of Remaining* (Louisville, KY: Westminster John Knox Press, 2010), 3.

2. Judith Herman, *Trauma and Recovery: The Aftermath of Violence —from Domestic Abuse to Political Terror* (New York: Basic Books, 1997), 9.

3. "PTSD Overview," Veteran's Administration website, accessed August 25, 2017, https://www.ptsd.va.gov/professional/PTSD-overview/ptsd -overview.asp.

4. *Diagnostic and Statistical Manual of Mental Disorders*, 4th ed. (St. Louis: American Psychiatric Association, 1994), 427.

5. Paola Arnabodi, et al., "PTSD symptoms as a consequence of breast cancer diagnosis: clinical implications," *SpringerPlus* 3 (2014): 392.

6. *Diagnostic and Statistical Manual of Mental Disorders*, 5th ed. (Arlington, VA: American Psychiatric Publishing, 2013), 274.

7. In a 2017 study of women in Germany with breast cancer, stages 0–III, researchers discovered that as many as 82.5 percent of the patients initially showed breast-cancer-related symptoms of PTSD, and a year later, those symptoms had not resolved in 57.3 percent of those cases. See Varinka Voight, et al., "Clinically Assessed Posttraumatic Stress in Patients with Breast Cancer during the First Year after Diagnosis in the Prospective, Longitudinal, Controlled COGNICARES Study," *Psycho-Oncology* 26 (2017): 77.

8. Lindsay N. French-Rosas, M.D., Jennifer Moye, Ph.D., and Aanand D. Naik, M.D., "Improving the Recognition and Treatment of Cancer-Related Posttraumatic Stress Disorder," *Journal of Psychiatric Practice* 17, no. 4 (2011 July): 2.

9. Bessel van der Kolk, *The Body Keeps the Score: Brain, Mind, and Body in the Healing of Trauma* (New York: Viking Books, 2014), 68.

10. French-Rosas, et al., "Improving the Recognition," 2.

11. Ibid.

12. Van der Kolk, *Body Keeps the Score*, 90.

13. Rambo, *Spirit and Trauma*, 7.

14. Audre Lorde, *The Cancer Journals* (San Francisco: Aunt Lute Books, 1980), 55–65.

15. Studies vary in the percentages of women choosing reconstructive surgery after a mastectomy. The American Society of Plastic Surgeons reports a 35 percent increase since the year 2000 whereas one study in 2011 indicated that 63 percent of women who were candidates chose reconstruction. Other studies indicate that in some parts of the United States, the number is as high as 80 percent. See Roni Caryn Rabin, "'Going Flat' After Breast Cancer," *New York Times*, October 31, 2016, accessed February 2, 2017, https://www .nytimes.com/2016/11/01/well/live/going-flat-after-breast-cancer.html?_r=0.

16. Ibid.

17. Jason Micheli, *Cancer Is Funny: Keeping Faith in Stage-Serious Chemo* (Minneapolis: Fortress Press, 2016), 139.

18. Ibid., 132.

19. Ibid., 141.

20. "Cancer Treatment for Men: Possible Sexual Side Effects," Mayo Clinic, "Patient Care and Health Info,", accessed July 14, 2017, http://www .mayoclinic.org/diseases-conditions/cancer/in-depth/cancer-treatment/ART -20045422?pg=1.

21. Arthur Frank, *At the Will of the Body: Reflections on Illness* (Boston: Houghton Mifflin, 1991).

22. Rambo, *Spirit and Trauma*, 15.

23. Frank, *Will of the Body*, 65.

24. Frank, *Will of the Body*, 67.

25. Anne Hughes, Maria Gudmundsdottir, and Betty Davies, "Everyday Struggling to Survive: Experiences of the Urban Poor Living with Advanced Cancer," *Oncology Nursing Forum* 34, no. 6 (2007): 1118.

26. Frank, *Will of the Body*, 83.

27. See also Susan Sontag, *Illness as Metaphor and AIDS and Its Metaphors* (New York: Picador, 2001), which talks about the stigma associated with cancer.

28. Susan Sontag, *Illness as Metaphor* (New York: Farrar, Straus & Giroux, 1977), 86.

29. Ibid., 87.

30. Frank, *Will of the Body*, 138.

31. Rebecca Eileen Olson, "Managing Hope, Denial, or Temporal Anomie? Informal Cancer Carers' Accounts of Spouses' Cancer Diagnoses," *Social Science & Medicine* 73 (2011): 907.

32. French-Rosas, et al., "Improving the Recognition," 6.

33. This study of women diagnosed with breast cancer reports that 60–95 percent report post-traumatic growth after their diagnosis. They also acknowledge, "Our study relied on self-report measures and, as such, the

associations reported may be suspect due to common method variance." E. F. Morrill, et al., "The Interaction of Post-traumatic Growth and Post-traumatic Stress Symptoms in Predicting Depressive Symptoms and Quality of Life." *Psycho-Oncology* 17 (2008): 51.

34. Paul Kalanithi, *When Breath Becomes Air* (New York: Random House, 2016), 147.

35. French-Rosas, et al., "Improving the Recognition," 8.

36. Rebecca Eileen Olson, "Indefinite Loss: The Experiences of Carers of a Spouse with Cancer," *European Journal of Cancer Care* 23, no. 4 (July 2014): 23.

37. Rambo, *Spirit and Trauma*, 3.

38. Olson, "Indefinite Loss," 561.

39. Ibid., 557.

40. J. Todd Billings, *Rejoicing in Lament: Wrestling with Incurable Cancer and Life in Christ* (Grand Rapids: Baker Books, 2015), 151.

41. Frank, *Will of the Body*, 13.

42. Billings, *Rejoicing in Lament*, 150.

43. Van der Kolk, *Body Keeps the Score* , 17.

44. Frank, *Will of the Body*, 1–2.

45. Ibid., 43.

46. Carrie Host, *Between Me and the River: A Memoir* (New York: Harlequin, 2011), 119.

47. Ibid., 243.

48. French-Rosas, et al, "Improving the Recognition," 6.

49. Julie K. Silver, ed., *What Helped Get Me Through: Cancer Survivors Share Wisdom and Hope* (Atlanta: American Cancer Society, 2009), esp. chap. 11, "What I Wish I Had Known at Diagnosis," 203–26, which presents multiple statements about how people wished they could have talked with those who were further along the cancer path than they were.

50. Rambo, *Spirit and Trauma*, 15.

51. Billings, *Rejoicing in Lament*, 109.

52. Van der Kolk, *Body Keeps the Score*, 243.

53. Christian Wiman, *My Bright Abyss: Meditations of a Modern Believer* (New York: Farrar, Straus & Giroux, 2013).

54. Deborah van Deusen Hunsinger, *Bearing the Unbearable: Trauma, Gospel, and Pastoral Care* (Grand Rapids: Wm. B. Eerdmans Publishing Co., 2016), 8.

55. Nicholas Wolterstorff, *Lament for a Son* (Grand Rapids: Wm. B. Eerdmans Publishing Co., 1987), 74.

56. David A. Carp, *Speaking of Sadness: Depression, Disconnection, and Meanings of Illness*, 20th anniversary ed. (Oxford: Oxford University Press, 2016), 71.

Carp relies here on studies of those who live with epilepsy, childhood leukemia, and multiple sclerosis. Also see J. Schneider and P. Conrad, "In the Closet with Epilepsy: Epilepsy, Stigma Potential and Information Control"; and J. Comaroff and P. Maguire, "Ambiguity and the Search for Meaning: Childhood Leukemia in the Modern Clinical Context"; both in *The Sociology of Health and Illness*, ed. P. Conrad and R. Kern (New York: St. Martin's, 1986); and D. Stewart and T. Sullivan, "Illness Behavior and the Sick Role in Chronic Disease: The Case of Multiple Sclerosis," *Social Science and Medicine* 16 (1982): 1397–404.

57. *Diagnostic and Statistical Manual of Mental Disorders*, 4th ed., text rev. (Washington, DC: American Psychiatric Association, 2000), 274.

58. Olson, "Managing Hope," 905.

59. Wiman, *Bright Abyss*, 56.

60. Olson, "Managing Hope," 907.

61. Ibid.

62. Ibid., 555–56.

63. Heide Goetze, et al., "Predictors of Quality of Life of Cancer Patients, Their Children, and Partners," *Psycho-oncology* 24, no. 7 (July 2015): 788.

64. Ibid., 793.

65. Olson, "Managing Hope," 909.

66. Herman, *Trauma and Recovery*, 211.

67. Kristin A. Loiselle, et al., "Posttraumatic Growth Associated with a Relative's Serious Illness," *Family Systems Health* 29, no. 1 (March 2011): 6. While this article focuses on relatives of those living with a serious illness, the findings on post-traumatic growth apply not just to relatives but to those experiencing "challenging life events" (6).

68. Maria Karekla and Marios Constantinou, "Religious Coping and Cancer: Proposing an Acceptance and Commitment Therapy Approach," *Cognitive and Behavioral Practice* 17 (2010): 372.

69. Ibid., 372.

70. Ibid., 376.

Chapter 3: Trauma, Illness, and the Christian Story

1. Serene Jones, *Trauma and Grace: Theology in a Ruptured World* (Louisville, KY: Westminster John Knox Press, 2009).

2. Ibid., 155.

3. Kathleen Billman and Daniel Migliore, *Rachel's Cry: Prayer of Lament and Rebirth of Hope* (Cleveland, OH: United Church Press, 1999), 25.

4. Maria Karekla and Marios Constantinou, "Religious Coping and Cancer: Proposing an Acceptance and Commitment Therapy Approach," *Cognitive and Behavioral Practice* 17 (2010): 373.

5. Thomas G. Long, *What Shall We Say? Evil, Suffering, and The Crisis of Faith* (Grand Rapids: Wm. B. Eerdmans Publishing Co., 2011), 52. I adapted Long's musings "I see that the wicked prosper. I wonder if there's a God? and O God, why do the wicked prosper?" to make the point specifically about illness.

6. Julie J. Exline, Kalman J. Kaplan, and Joshua B. Grubbs, "Anger, Exit, and Assertion: Do People See Protest toward God as Morally Acceptable?" *Psychology of Religion and Spirituality* 4 (2012): 274.

7. Billman and Migliore, *Rachel's Cry*, 25.

8. Susan Gubar, *Memoir of a Debulked Woman: Ending Ovarian Cancer* (New York: W. W. Norton & Co., 2012), 155.

9. Elaine Scarry, *Body in Pain: The Making and Unmaking of the World* (London: Oxford University Press, 1987), 4.

10. Billman and Migliore, *Rachel's Cry*, 25, 109.

11. Jones, *Trauma and Grace*, 52.

12. Deborah van Deusen Hunsinger, *Bearing the Unbearable: Trauma, Gospel, and Pastoral Care* (Grand Rapids: Wm. B. Eerdmans Publishing Co., 2016), 83–85.

13. Billman and Migliore, *Rachel's Cry*, 29.

14. "Though it is not beyond imagination that one person could suffer all these problems, I expect at least some of the language is metaphoric," writes Glenn Pemberton in *Hurting with God: Learning to Lament with the Psalms* (Abilene, TX: Abilene Christian University Press, 2012), 106.

15. Frederick J. Gaiser, *Healing in the Bible: Theological Insight for Christian Ministry* (Grand Rapids: Baker Academic, 2010), 76.

16. Ibid., 74.

17. Christian Wiman, *My Bright Abyss: Meditations of a Modern Believer* (New York: Farrar, Straus & Giroux, 2013), 148.

18. Gaiser, *Healing in the Bible*, 76.

19. Ibid., 77–78.

20. Jones, *Trauma and Grace*, 57.

21. Ibid.

22. Gaiser, *Healing in the Bible*, 82.

23. Karekla and Constantinou, "Religious Coping," 376.

24. Gaiser, *Healing in the Bible*, 9.

25. Ibid., 16.

26. Kathryn Greene-McCreight, *Darkness Is My Only Companion: A Christian Response to Mental Illness* (Grand Rapids: Brazos Press, 2015), 162.

27. Piet Zuidgeest, *The Absence of God: Exploring the Christian Tradition in a Situation of Mourning* (Boston: Brill, 2001), 133.

28. Ibid., 134.

29. Greene-McCreight, *Darkness*, 29.

30. Ibid., 160.

31. J. Todd Billings, *Rejoicing in Lament: Wrestling with Incurable Cancer and Life in Christ* (Grand Rapids: Baker Books, 2015).

32. Ibid, 38.

33. Ibid.

34. Bessel van der Kolk, *The Body Keeps the Score: Brain, Mind, and Body in the Healing of Trauma* (New York: Viking Books, 2014), 90.

35. Hunsinger, *Bearing the Unbearable*, 91.

36. Jason Micheli, interviewed by Jana Reiss, "Flunking Sainthood," December 30, 2016, accessed May 1, 2017, http://religionnews.com/2016/12 /30/cancer-is-funny-says-pastor-and-his-writing-makes-it-so/.

37. See Thomas Long's discussion of Peter L. Berger's view of theodicy and nomos in Long, *What Shall We Say?* 55, referencing Berger's *The Sacred Canopy: Elements of a Sociological Theory of Religion* (New York: Anchor Books, 1969), 54–55.

38. Hunsinger, *Bearing the Unbearable*, 92.

39. *The Lutheran Study Bible—NRSV* (Minneapolis: Augsburg Fortress, 2009), 790.

40. Ilana Pardes, "Wife of Job: Bible," *Jewish Women: A Comprehensive Historical Encyclopedia*, March 1, 2009, Jewish Women's Archive, accessed July 11, 2017, https://jwa.org/encyclopedia/article/wife-of-job-bible.

41. *Lutheran Study Bible*, 792.

42. Shelly Rambo, *Spirit and Trauma: A Theology of Remaining* (Louisville, KY: Westminster John Knox Press, 2010), 3.

43. David B. Burrell, *Deconstructing Theodicy: Why Job Has Nothing to Say to the Puzzle of Suffering* (Grand Rapids: Brazos Press, 2008), 32.

44. Hunsinger, *Bearing the Unbearable*, 92.

45. James L. Kugel, *In the Valley of the Shadow: On the Foundations of Religious Belief* (New York: Free Press, 2011), 144–45.

46. As cited in Julie K. Silver, ed., *What Helped Get Me Through: Cancer Survivors Share Wisdom and Hope* (Atlanta: American Cancer Society, 2009), 222.

47. Hunsinger, *Bearing the Unbearable*, 95.

48. Daniel Castelo, "First World Theodical Problems," unpublished essay delivered to the faculty of Western Theological Seminary and Hope College, March 3, 2017, 14.

49. Ibid., 15.

50. Long, *What Shall We Say?*, 107.

51. Michael E. W. Thompson, *Where Is the God of Justice? The Old Testament and Suffering* (Eugene, OR: Pickwick Publications, 2011), 147.

52. Ibid., 164.

53. Burrell, *Deconstructing Theodicy*, 18.

54. S. Fuller, R. Clements, and C. H. Swenson, "Stages of Religious Faith and Reactions to Terminal Cancer," *Journal of Psychology and Theology* 21 (Fall 1993): 242, 245.

55. This study of patients diagnosed with a brain tumor or multiple sclerosis between 2001–2006 showed that if gender is not isolated, the rate of divorce for those living with one of these illnesses is on par with the general population. But if one controls for gender, women are seven times more likely to be abandoned by their partners in the midst of dealing with one of these illnesses than are men. See Michael J. Glantz, et al., "Gender Disparity in the Rate of Partner Abandonment in Patients with Serious Medical Illness," *Cancer: Journal of the American Cancer Society* 115, no. 22 (November 2009): 5237–242.

56. Carol Newsom, *The Book of Job: A Contest of Moral Imagination* (Oxford: Oxford University Press, 2003), 257–58.

57. Hunsinger, *Bearing the Unbearable*, 1.

58. Maia Kotrosits and Hal Taussig, *Re-Reading the Gospel of Mark amidst Loss and Trauma* (New York: Palgrave Macmillan, 2013), 4.

59. Ibid., 20.

60. Ibid., 46.

61. See the intriguing chapter by Adele Reinhartz, "The Destruction of the Jerusalem Temple as a Trauma for Nascent Christianity," in *Trauma and Traumatization in Individual and Collective Dimensions: Insights from Biblical Studies and Beyond*, ed. Eve-Marie Becker, Jan Dochhorn, and Else Holt (Göttingen, Ger.: Vandenhoeck & Ruprecht, 2014), accessed June 15, 2017, https://www.academia.edu/20285183/The_Destruction_of_the_Jerusalem_Temple_as_a_Trauma_for_Nascent_Christianity.

62 Flavius Josephus, *The Wars of the Jews, or History of the Destruction of Jerusalem*, 6.1.1, trans. William Whiston, Christians Classics Ethereal Library, accessed August 28, 2017, http://www.ccel.org/j/josephus/works/war-6.htm.

63. Kotrosits and Taussig, *Re-Reading the Gospel of Mark*, 129–30.

64. See William Placher's discussion of this passage in *Mark*, Belief: A Theological Commentary on the Bible, ed. William Placher and Amy Plantinga Pauw (Louisville, KY: Westminster John Knox Press, 2010), 233.

65. Placher, *Mark*, 236.

66. Morna Hooker, *The Gospel According to St. Mark: Black's New Testament Commentary* (London: A & C Black, 1991), 375.

67. See Fleming Rutledge's extensive argument on this point in Fleming Rutledge, *The Crucifixion: Understanding the Death of Jesus Christ* (Grand Rapids: Wm. B. Eerdmans Publishing Co., 2015), 197.

68. Jones, *Trauma and Grace*, 77, 81.

69. Christian Wiman, *My Bright Abyss: Meditations of a Modern Believer* (New York: Farrar, Straus & Giroux, 2013), 106–7.

70. Christian Wiman, speaking in "A Poet and a Theologian Discuss Incurable Cancer—Christian Wiman and Todd Billings," Western Theological Seminary's James I. Cook Endowment in Christianity & Literature and the Osterhaven Lecture Series, March 31, 2015, accessed February 20, 2017, http://jtoddbillings.com/2015/03/penetratingly-honest-and-expansively-hopeful/.

71. Wiman, *Bright Abyss*, 133.

72. Jones, *Trauma and Grace*, 88.

73. Ibid., 89.

74. Ibid.

75. Alan E. Lewis, *Between Cross and Resurrection: A Theology of Holy Saturday* (Grand Rapids: Wm. B. Eerdmans Publishing Co., 2003), 1.

76. Ibid., 31.

77. Ibid., 44.

78. Ibid., 37.

79. Wayne Grudem, "He Did Not Descend into Hell: A Plea for Following Scripture instead of the Apostles' Creed," *Journal of the Evangelical Theological Society* 34, no. 1 (March 1991): 103–13, accessed July 24, 2017, http://www.waynegrudem.com/wp-content/uploads/2012/08/he-did-not-descend-into-hell_JETS.pdf.

80. Shelly Rambo, *Spirit and Trauma: A Theology of Remaining* (Louisville, KY: Westminster John Knox Press, 2010), 50.

81. Ibid.; see also Adrienne von Speyr and Hans Urs von Balthasar, *Kreutz und Hölle* (Einsiedeln: Johannes Verlag, 1966), 86–115, as cited in ibid.

82. See Fleming Rutledge's engaging discussion of biblical depictions of hell (Rutledge, *Crucifixion*, 398–408).

83. Ibid., 450.

84. Jones, *Trauma and Grace*, 148.

85. I am indebted to Shelly Rambo (author of *Spirit and Trauma*) for this image of the womb becoming a tomb.

86. Robert Jenson, *Systematic Theology: The Works of God*, vol. 2 (Oxford: Oxford University Press, 2001), 331.

87. Rutledge, *Crucifixion*, 461.

88. Jones, *Trauma and Grace*, 149.

89. Ibid., 150.

90. Rambo, *Spirit and Trauma*, 79.

91. Hunsinger, *Bearing the Unbearable*, 40, endnote 37.

92. Ibid., 2.

93. Billings, "Poet and Theologian Discuss."

94. Jason Micheli, *Cancer Is Funny: Keeping Faith in Stage-Serious Chemo* (Minneapolis: Fortress Press, 2016), 150.

Chapter 4: Church for the Undone

1. Jason Micheli, *Cancer Is Funny: Keeping Faith in Stage-Serious Chemo* (Minneapolis: Fortress Press, 2016), 162.

2. See Martin Luther's *Large Catechism*, in Paul T. McCain, ed., *Concordia: The Lutheran Confessions: A Reader's Edition of the Book of Concord*, 2nd ed. (St. Louis: Concordia Publishing House, 2005), paras. 83–84, http://bookofconcord.org/lc-6-baptism.php.

3. Micheli, *Cancer Is Funny*, 161.

4. JoAnn A. Post, *Songs in My Head: A Cancer Spiritual* (Eugene, OR: Wipf & Stock, 2015), 12.

5. Ibid., 13.

6. JoAnn Post, "Open to That," unpublished essay, May 16, 2017.

7. Michael Frost, *Incarnate: The Body of Christ in an Age of Disengagement* (Downers Grove, IL: InterVarsity Press, 2014), 208.

8. Bessel van der Kolk, *The Body Keeps the Score: Brain, Mind, and Body in the Healing of Trauma* (New York: Viking Books, 2014), see esp. chs. 14, 18, and 20.

9. A helpful discussion of what ritual can accomplish for those who experience a sense of chaos, disorder, and lack of meaning in their lives due to aging can be found in Dayle A. Friedman, "An Anchor amidst the *Anomie*: Ritual and Aging," *Aging, Spirituality, and Religion: A Handbook*, vol. 2, ed. Melvin Kimble and Susan McFadden (Minneapolis: Fortress Press, 2002), esp. 136–37.

10. Kathleen Billman and Daniel Migliore, *Rachel's Cry: Prayer of Lament and Rebirth of Hope* (Cleveland, OH: United Church Press, 1999), 137.

11. J. Todd Billings, *Rejoicing in Lament: Wrestling with Incurable Cancer and Life in Christ* (Grand Rapids: Baker Books, 2015), 40. See also Glenn Pemberton's discussion of contemporary Christian aversion to lament in *Hurting with God: Learning to Lament with the Psalms* (Abilene, TX: Abilene Christian University Press, 2012), 35–41.

12. Billings, *Rejoicing in Lament*, 40–41.

13. Julie J. Exline, Kalman J. Kaplan, and Joshua B. Grubbs, "Anger, Exit, and Assertion: Do People See Protest toward God as Morally Acceptable?" *Psychology of Religion and Spirituality* 4 (2012): 274.

14. Ibid.

15. Billman and Migliore, *Rachel's Cry*, 86–87.

16. Deanna A. Thompson, *Hoping for More: Having Cancer, Talking Faith, and Accepting Grace* (Eugene, OR: Cascade Books, 2012), 63.

17. Patricia Lull, "What Kind of Christian?" *Lutheran Women Today* (May 2009): 24.

18. Stanley Hauerwas, "Salvation and Health: Why Medicine Needs the Church," in *On Moral Medicine: Theological Perspectives on Medical Ethics*, ed. Stephen Lammers, et al., 2nd ed. (Grand Rapids: Wm. B. Eerdmans Publishing Co., 1998), 82.

19. Parker Palmer, *Let Your Life Speak: Listening for the Voice of Vocation* (San Francisco: Jossey Bass, 2000), 57.

20. Ibid., 64.

21. Hauerwas, "Salvation and Health," 82.

22. Ibid, 82.

23. I am indebted to JoAnn Post for the insight regarding the differences between a ministry of presence and a ministry of silence.

24. Jann Aldredge-Clanton, *Counseling People with Cancer* (Louisville, KY: Westminster John Knox Press, 1998), 22.

25. Maria Karekla and Marios Constantinou, "Religious Coping and Cancer: Proposing an Acceptance and Commitment Therapy Approach," *Cognitive and Behavioral Practice* 17 (2010): 371.

26. Aldredge-Clanton, *Counseling People with Cancer*, 54.

27. Deanna A. Thompson, *The Virtual Body of Christ in a Suffering World* (Nashville: Abingdon Press, 2016).

28. See my discussion of live-streaming worship and other ways of incorporating those who are unable to get to church into the life of the church through virtual means (ibid., 92–96).

29. Theresa of Avila, "Christ Has No Body but Yours," accessed March 26, 2018, https://www.journeywithjesus.net/PoemsAndPrayers/Teresa_Of_Avila_Christ_Has_No_Body.shtml.

30. Frederick J. Gaiser, *Healing in the Bible: Theological Insight for Christian Ministry* (Grand Rapids: Baker Academic, 2010), 173.

31. Ibid., 174.

32. Nancy Eiesland, *The Disabled God: Toward a Liberatory Theology of Disability* (Nashville: Abingdon Press, 1994), 117.

33. Billings, *Rejoicing in Lament*, 113.

34. Gaiser, *Healing in the Bible*, 250.

35. Ibid., 238.

36. Micheli, *Cancer Is Funny*, 87–88.

37. Ibid., 169.

38. Christopher Hitchens, "Miss Manners and the Big 'C'," *Vanity Fair*, December 2010, accessed June 28, 2017, http://www.vanityfair.com/news /2010/12/hitchens-201012.

39. Dirk Lange, *Trauma Recalled: Liturgy, Disruption, and Theology* (Minneapolis: Fortress Press, 2009), 177.

Chapter 5: Not-Yet-Resurrection Hope

1. Rebecca Solnit, *Hope in the Dark: Untold Histories, Wild Possibilities* (New York: Nation Books, 2004), 4.

2. Bessel van der Kolk, *The Body Keeps the Score: Brain, Mind, and Body in the Healing of Trauma* (New York: Viking Books, 2014), 30.

3. It is unknown what the "physical infirmity" was that Paul references in Gal. 4:13. Some think it was some kind of illness while others suggest it was related to the persecution he suffered (Harold W. Attridge, Society of Biblical Literature, *HarperCollins Study Bible—New Revised Standard Version* [New York: HarperCollins, 2006], 1978).

4. Solnit, *Hope in the Dark*, 27.

5. Ibid., 16.

6. Ibid., 23.

7. Biblical scholars differ on their views of the reasons for the deaths in the Thessalonian community as well as reasons for the grief. While some suggest that the deaths are linked to persecution (influenced by the discussion in Acts 17 about the unrest in Thessalonica during Paul's visit), I'm persuaded by Beverly Gaventa's claims that the anticipated persecution of the Thessalonian Christians (referenced in 1 Thess. 3:3) has more to do with Paul's apocalyptic sensibilities throughout this letter than with actual persecutions that have already occurred. Therefore, Gaventa argues, the most likely reason for the anxiety surrounding the death of their fellow Christians is that they did not expect anyone to die before Christ's return: "The deaths of believers have now occurred, however, prompting a trauma." Paul writes to this context to comfort them. See Beverly Roberts Gaventa, *First and Second Thessalonians*, Interpretation: A Bible Commentary for Teaching and Preaching (Louisville, KY: Westminster John Knox Press, 1998), 63.

8. See, for example, Florence Morgan Gillman, Mary Ann Beavis, and HyeRan Kim-Cragg, *1–2 Thessalonians*, Wisdom Commentary, vol. 52 (Collegeville, MN: Liturgical Press, 2016), 77–78.

9. Attridge, *HarperCollins Study Bible*, 2,009.

10. Jann Aldredge-Clanton, *Counseling People with Cancer* (Louisville, KY: Westminster John Knox Press, 1998), 41.

11. Paul Kalanithi, *When Breath Becomes Air* (New York: Random House, 2016), 134.

12. Several people interviewed expressed a version of this sentiment when asked what they'd wish they'd known at diagnosis. See Julie K. Silver, ed., *What Helped Get Me Through: Cancer Survivor's Share Wisdom and Hope* (Atlanta: American Cancer Society, 2009), 213.

13. Frederick J. Gaiser, *Healing in the Bible: Theological Insight for Christian Ministry* (Grand Rapids: Baker Academic, 2010), 240.

14. Conversation with Andy Tix, July 12, 2017.

15. Obituary of Leslie Nelson Tengwall, accessed July 15, 2017, http://www.startribune.com/obituaries/detail/206929/?fullname=leslie-nelson-tengwall.

16. Aldredge-Clanton, *Counseling People with Cancer*, 54.

17 Wolterstorff, *Lament for a Son*, 101–2.

18. Daniel Migliore, *Faith Seeking Understanding: An Introduction to Christian Theology*, 2nd ed. (Grand Rapids: Wm. B. Eerdmans Publishing Co., 2004) 340.

19. Laura Nasrallah, "Empire and Apocalypse in Thessaloniki: Interpreting the Early Christian Rotunda," *Journal of Early Christian Studies* 13 (2005): 500, as quoted in Gillman, et al., *1–2 Thessalonians*, 78.

20. Ibid., 78.

21. As cited in Hans Schwartz, "Eschatology," *Christian Dogmatics*, vol. 2, ed. Carl E. Braaten and Robert W. Jenson (Philadelphia: Fortress Press, 1984), 586.

22. Martin Luther, *Kritische Gesamtausgabe*, vol. 5 (Weimar, Germany, 1883), 191, as cited by Walther von Loewenich, *Martin Luther: The Man and His Work*, trans. Lawrence Denef (Philadelphia: Fortress Press, 1986), 285.

23. David Jenson, *Living Hope: The Future and Christian Faith* (Louisville, KY: Westminster John Knox Press, 2010), 33.

24. Ibid., 34.

25. Ibid., 41.

26. Camille Scheel, *Camp Chemo: Postcards Home from Metastatic Breast Cancer* (Edina, MN: Beaver's Pond Press, 2015), 246.

27. I am indebted to Shelly Rambo for this insight of rediscovering a rhythm.

INDEX

abandonment by God, 66, 74, 93, 104–5

absence of God, 40, 83–85, 105–6, 133

acceptance, of diagnosis, 33

Aldredge-Clanton, Jann, 132–35, 152, 153

alone, feeling of, 66, 83–84

anger
  and breast cancer, 26
  divine, 82, 84
  at God, 70, 75, 125–26 (*see also* lamentation)
  in Job, 99
  psalms, language in, 87
  in worship, 126

anomie
  about, 4–5
  in cancer stories, 13–15
  in health, control of, 29
  and Holy Saturday, 108, 116–18
  and lamentation, 126
  temporal, 67–69
  of worship, 124–25

anomos, 4, 143

antidepressants, 58

Apostles' Creed, 109

appearances, keeping up, 55

Ash Wednesday, 127

atheists, 105

At the Will of the Body: Reflections on Illness (Frank), 54, 56

attitude, of the ill, 26–29

baptism, 101, 120–22

Bearing the Unbearable: Trauma, Gospel, and Pastoral Care (Hunsinger), 65

Beckett, Samuel, 14, 16

Being Mortal: Medicine and What Matters in the End (Gewande), 12

Berger, Peter, 89

Bible
  Acts, 138
  Exodus, 84
  1 Corinthians
    chapter 5: 110
    chapter 11: 146
    chapter 12: 120–21
    chapter 15: 66, 104, 113
  1 Peter, 110
  1 Thessalonians
    chapter 4: 149, 154–57, 160
    See also Paul: on eschaton; Paul: on hope
  Galatians
    chapter 3: 121
    chapter 6: 129

Bible (*continued*)
  Genesis
    chapter 2: 78
    chapter 3: 127
  Isaiah, 156
  Jeremiah
    chapter 31: 73
  Job
    chapter 1: 90
    chapter 2: 90–92
    chapter 3: 91
    chapter 4: 93
    chapter 7: 93
    chapter 8: 93
    chapter 10: 78, 94
    chapter 11: 93
    chapter 12: 94
    chapter 13: 95
    chapter 38: 95
    chapter 39: 98
    chapter 40: 96
    chapter 42: 96–97
  Joel, 156
  John, 108
  Luke (Gospel of)
    chapter 22: 145
    chapter 23: 108
    chapter 24: 116–17
  Mark (Gospel of)
    chapter 10: 120
    chapter 15: 103, 105, 108
  Matthew (Gospel of)
    chapter 27: 103, 105, 108
    chapter 28: 120
  Psalm
    chapter 6: 36, 81–83
    chapter 8: 76
    chapter 27: 86–87
    chapter 38: 77–81
    chapter 77: 76
    chapter 88: 83–86
    chapter 113: 76
    See also psalms

Romans
  chapter 1: 115
  chapter 6: 121
1 Corinthians
  chapter 12: 120
2 Peter, 110
Revelation
  chapter 21: 157
Billings, Todd, 31–37, 60–62, 85, 87, 116, 125
Billman, Kathleen, 73, 75–77, 126
blood cancer, 37
bodies, during eschaton, 156–58
body keeping score. *See* body-self connection; deterioration, of bodies
Body Keeps the Score: Brain, Mind, and Body in the Healing of Trauma, The (van der Kolk), 47, 64, 124
body of Christ, 119–21, 129–30, 140–41
body-self connection
  about, 7, 41
  and cancer stories, 16–21
  and healing, 138–39
  in Job, 89–99
  in men, 51–52
  in the psalms, 76, 78–79, 82, 86–87
bone-marrow biopsy, 38
Boss, Pauline, 5
Bowler, Kate, 25–27, 71
breast cancer
  author's, 1
  culture of, 23–24
  and mastectomies, 20–21, 49–51, 53–54
  and reconstructive surgery, 50–51
burdens, bearing one another's, 129–30
Burrell, David, 97
Butler, Judith, 41

Calvin, John, 79–80
cancer and ministry. *See* trauma and ministry
cancers
  blood, 37
  breast (*see* breast cancer)
  colon, 25–26
  lung, 14, 59
  metastatic carcinoid, 19
  multiple myeloma, 32, 60
  ovarian, 17–19
cancer stories
  about, 11–14
  and community, 21–23
  of deterioration of bodies, 16–21
  and faith, 37–39
  and the future, 31–35
  God in, 39–41
  and hopelessness, 14–16
  importance of, 13–14
  lamentation in, 35–37
  positivity in, 13, 23–27
  realistic, 27–31, 53
caregivers, 94–95
Caruth, Cathy, 41–42
Castelo, Daniel, 95
cell division, 18
chaplains, role with the ill, 132–33
chemotherapy, 21–22, 57
child, loss of, 112, 114
Christ. *See* Jesus Christ
Christian story. *See* theology, of trauma
chronic conditions. *See* illnesses
church, beginning of, 117
church, for the suffering
  and baptism, 120–22
  bringing comfort, 129–32
  communion in, 144–46
  and healing, 137–40
  lamentation in, 124–29
  and others' suffering, 140–44

and technology, 135–37
  and worship attendance, 122–24
church service. *See* worship
city imagery, 157
colon cancer, 25–26
comfort, from the well to the ill, 129–32, 154, 160–61
Communion (sacrament), 144–46
community, 18–19, 22–23. *See also* church, for the suffering
control, God in, 80–81, 96. *See also* nomos
counselors, cancer, 2, 53–54
creation story, 66, 112
Crucified God, The (Moltmann), 106
crucifixion. *See also* Holy Saturday; resurrection
  about, 100
  and the cry from the cross, 103–7
  and lamentation, 128
  Mark on, 102–4
  and trauma parallels, 104–5
  wounds of, 158
cry from the cross, Jesus, 103–7

death
  of child, 112, 114
  and creation story, 66, 112
  end of, 157
  as enemy, final, 113
  fear of, 61
  knowledge of, 12
  life beyond, 150–52 (*see also* eschaton)
  likelihood of, 59–60
  trauma likened to, 50
debulking, 17–18
depression, 55, 58–59
deterioration, of bodies, 17–22, 34–35, 38
disorder. *See* anomie
dreams, about cancer, 6

edification, because of illness, 25–26, 39, 55

Ehrenreich, Barbara, 23–31, 53, 88, 89, 92–94

Eiesland, Nancy, 138–39

emotional work, 54–55

emotions, in illnesses. *See* body-self connection

encouragement, 160–61

eschaton
bodies, during, 156–58
and hope, 155
Paul on, 149, 155–56

evil, moral, 44, 64–65, 100–101, 105, 110–11

Exline, Julie, 75, 126

faith, 37–39, 66, 139, 157

families, 66–69, 128–29, 143

Fault in Our Stars (Green), 7

fault, feeling of being at, 29

fear, 55, 61, 82, 148–50

feast (sacrament), 144–46

fight, 56–57. *See also* warrior imagery

Final Judgment. *See* eschaton

financial planning, 67

flat, go, 51

forgiveness, 144–46

forsakenness, 39–40, 105–6

Frank, Arthur, 8, 13, 18, 54, 56–58, 60

friends
Christ-like, 95
Jesus, 103
in Job, 92–97, 131–32
loss of, 94
suffering of, 67–68

future, redefining, 31–35, 59–64, 100–107, 149–50

Gaiser, Frederick, 78, 81, 138, 140, 152–53

genocide, 110–11

Gewande, Atul, 12

gift, cancer as, 25. *See also* positivity, in cancer stories

Gillan, Florence, 156

God
abandonment by, 66, 74, 93, 104–5, 133
absence of, 40, 83–85, 105–6, 133
anger at, 70, 75, 125–26 (*see also* lamentation)
in cancer stories, 32–33, 36
comforted by, 114
in control, 80–81, 96
existence of, questioning, 74, 133
in illnesses, 25, 82
as parent, 112, 114
and suffering, 4, 39–41
trustworthiness of, 81, 86, 157–58

godforsakenness, 39–40, 105–6

go on. *See* perseverance

Gospels, 100–101. *See also individual books*

Green, John, 7

Greene-McCreight, Kathryn, 84–86

grief, 55, 85, 112, 151–54, 158. *See also* lamentation

Gubar, Susan, 17–23, 30–31, 48, 76, 92

guilt, 66–68, 133

hands, laying of, 138–39

hate, of well toward ill, 131

Hauerwas, Stanley, 130–31

healing, 82–83, 101, 115, 137–40, 152–53

health, control of, 29

heart disease, 56–57

Hell, 109–11

Herman, Judith, 44, 69, 80

Hitchens, Christopher, 142–44

Holy Communion, 144–46

Holy Saturday
  about, 108–9
  and child death metaphor, 112–14
  and Hell, 109–11
  and the Holy Spirit, 114–15
Holy Spirit, 114–15
Hooker, Morna, 104
hope
  about, 147–48
  in death, 153
  and eschaton, 154–60
  and faith, 139
  and fear, 148–50
  and grief, 150–54
  language of, 155, 161
  need for, 68–69, 73–74
  Paul on, 151, 154–55, 161
  in the psalms, 81, 86
  through stories, 15, 134
  and trust, 148–50
Host, Carrie, 19–20, 35, 61–62
Hunsinger, Deborah, 77, 94,
    99–100, 115
hymnals, 125

identity, of the ill, 69
ileostomy, 18
illnesses
  in Bible (*see* pain, biblical stories of)
  and emotions (*see* body-self
    connection)
  God in, 25, 82
  and mind (*see* body-self
    connection)
  of others, recognizing, 140–42
  in post-traumatic stress disorder
    (PTSD) definition, 45
  sin, as punishment for, 69–70,
    78–79, 88, 93–94
  sociology of, 54–55
  technology for, 135–37
  trauma related (*see* trauma,
    illness-related)

immune systems, 28
immunotherapy, 28, 57
incarnation, 52
indefinite loss, 59–60, 68
internal threats, of trauma, 66. *See
    also* body-self connection
intimacy, 51–52
irresolution, 115–17. *See also* anomie
isolation, feeling of, 66, 83–84
Israelites, ancient, 75–76, 78–79, 88,
    93–94

Jenson, David, 158
Jenson, Robert, 113
Jeremiah, 73
Jesus Christ
  abandonment of, 103, 105
  baptism of, 101, 120
  crucifixion of (*see* crucifixion)
  cry from the cross, 103–7
  and death, 36
  and the Gospels, 100–101
  healings by, 138
  and Last Supper, 145
  Mark on, 101–4, 106–7
  and pain, 39–40
  resurrection of (*see* resurrection)
  second coming of (*see* eschaton)
  as Son of God, 102–4
  transfiguration of, 102
Job
  about, 89–91
  friends of, 92–97, 131–32
  lamentation, physical depiction
    of, 125
  reading post-diagnosis, 134
  restoration, 98–99
  spouse of, 91, 98
Jones, Serene, 72–73, 76–77, 80,
    104–7, 112, 114
Josephus, Flavius, 102
joy, during treatments, 22
Jude, 110

judgement day. *See* eschaton
justice, 72, 89

Kalanithi, Paul, 11–12, 14, 59, 152
Kolk, Bessel van der. *See* van der
    Kolk, Bessel
Kostrosits, Maia, 101–3
Kugel, James, 93–94

lamentation
    Jeremiah 31 (Rachel story),
        73–74
    making space for, 35–37
    in the psalms, 36, 76–77, 80
    in worship, 124–29
Lange, Dirk, 145
language
    cancer, 30–32, 35–36, 56–58
    of hope, 155, 161
    survivor, 30–31
    trauma, 54, 88, 124–25, 133
    victim, 56, 111
    of the well to the ill, 130
Last Supper, 145
laying of hands, 138–39
Lent, 127–28
Lewis, Alan, 108
life expectancy, 59–60, 68–69, 152,
    159
Long, Thomas, 74, 96
Lorde, Audre, 20–21, 49, 51
Lord's Prayer, 36
Lord's Supper, 145
Lull, Patricia, 129
lung cancer, 14, 59
Luther, Martin, 120, 157–58

malice, 44, 100–101, 105, 110–11
Mark (Gospel of)
    about, 101–2
    on crucifixion, 102–4
    ending of, 106–7
    and the resurrection, 106
marriages. *See* spouses, of the ill

Mary Magdalene, 106–7
masculinity, 51–52
mastectomies, 20–21, 49–51, 53–54
meaning, to suffering. *See* why,
    asking
medical treatment, rejecting, 69, 139
Memoir of a Debulked Woman
    (Gubar), 17
mental health, 53, 58, 83–86. *See also*
    post-traumatic stress disor-
    der (PTSD)
metastatic carcinoid cancer, 19
Micheli, Jason, 51–52, 88–89, 117,
    121, 141–42
Migliore, Daniel, 73, 75–77, 126, 155
military images, in cancer, 4, 30,
    56–57, 153, 156
mind, and illness. *See* body-self
    connection
ministers, role with ill, 132–33
ministry. *See* trauma and ministry
miscarriages, 112, 114
Moltmann, Jürgen, 106
moral evil, 44, 64–65, 100–101, 105,
    110–11
mortality, 12, 14, 38
multiple myeloma, 32, 60
*My Bright Abyss: Meditation of a Mod-
    ern Believer* (Wiman), 38

Nasrallah, Laura, 155
Newsom, Carol, 98
nomos
    about, 4
    faith as, 39
    in God's story, 87
    in Job, 97
    and why, asking, 26–27
    See also anomie

obituaries, 153
Olson, Rebecca, 59, 67–68
ovarian cancer, 17–19

pain
  and Jesus, 39–40
  and prayer, 75–76, 86–87
  in Scripture (*see* pain, biblical
    stories of)
  of treatments, 18, 20–22, 38,
    51–52
  See also suffering
pain, biblical stories of
  crucifixion
  Job (*see* Bible, Job)
  Psalm 6: 81–83
  Psalm 38: 77–81
  Psalm 88: 83–85
Palmer, Parker, 130
parent, God as a, 112, 114
parenting, with cancer, 2, 26, 33–34,
  68
parish nurses, 153–54
parousia, 155–56. *See also* eschaton
passion story. *See* crucifixion
pastoral care, 132–33
Paul (the apostle)
  about, 148
  on baptism, 120–21
  on burdens, bearing one another's,
    129
  on church, 119–20
  on communion, 146
  on encouragement, 160–61
  on eschaton, 149, 155–56
  on hope, 151, 154–55, 161
penitential lament psalms, 77
perseverance
  because of community, 22–23
  and God, 39–41
  and lamentation, 35–37
  and language, realistic, 28–31
personality changes, 68
positive religious coping, 80
positivity, in cancer stories, 13,
  23–27
Post, JoAnn, 122–23, 127

post-traumatic stress disorder
  (PTSD), 5–7, 44–45, 47, 58
poverty, 55–56
praise, 76, 127. *See also* thanksgiving, giving
prayer, 33, 36, 37, 75–76, 86–88
processions, eschatological, 156
prognoses, 59, 68–69, 152, 159
psalms.
  about, 75–77, 127
  praying, 86–88
  in worship, 125
  See also Bible, Psalm
psychosocial therapy, 7
PTSD (post-traumatic stress disorder). *See* post-traumatic
  stress disorder (PTSD)
punishment, illnesses as, 69–70,
  78–79, 88, 93–94

*Rachel's Cry: Prayer of Lament and
  Rebirth of Hope* (Billman,
  Migliore), 73
Rambo, Shelly, 49–50, 59, 73,
  109–10, 114–15
rapture. *See* eschaton
*Reading and Writing Cancer: How
  Words Heal* (Gubar), 23
reason, cancer happens for a, 4, 26,
  34, 71. *See also* why, asking
reconstructive surgery (breast),
  50–51
re-creation, 155, 157. *See also*
  eschaton
recurrent cancer, 21–22
*Rejoicing in Lament: Wrestling with
  Incurable Cancer and Life in
  Christ* (Billings), 32–33, 36,
  116
relationships, 79, 160. *See also* families; friends
remission, 2–3, 35, 61–63
resolvability, 115–17

resurrection
    bodily, 149, 154–60
    and grief, 151–52
    in Luke, 116–17
    in Mark, 106
    not-yet, 139, 144–46
    and suffering, 121
rituals, religious, 124–25
Rufinus, Tyrannius, 109
Rutledge, Fleming, 110–11, 113–14

Satan, 90
Scarry, Elaine, 76
Scheel, Camille, 160
Schofield, Penelope, 28
second coming. *See* eschatonself-
    image, 51–52
sensory perceptions, during treat-
    ment, 48
sexual effects, of cancer, 51–52
sins
    Christ taking on, 110
    and death on cross, 104
    punishment for, 69–70, 78–79, 88,
        93–94
"Smile or Die: The Bright Side of
    Cancer" (Ehrenreich), 27
sociology, of illnesses, 54–55
Solnit, Rebecca, 149–50
Son of God, Jesus as, 102–4
Sontag, Susan, 57
Spirit, 114–15
spouses, of the ill, 51–52, 67–68, 91,
    98, 128, 142–43
statistics, on life expectancy, need
    for, 152
stem-cell transplants, 34–35
stigma, of cancer, 57
stillborn births, 112, 114
stories. *See* cancer stories
structure. *See* nomos
suffering
    as a death, 92

and God, 4, 39–41
    making sense of (*see* why, asking)
    meaning of, 39
    of others, recognizing, 140–42
    and resurrection, 121
    See also pain
support groups, 27, 62–63
surgeries
    back, 2
    debulking, 17–18
    mastectomies, 20–21, 49–51,
        53–54
    reconstructive, breast, 50–51
survivor language, 30–31
symptoms, of cancer, 17

Taussig, Hal, 101–3
technology, during illness, 135–37
temples, destruction of, 102
thanksgiving, giving, 76, 86, 87
theodicy, 89–90
theologians, with cancer, 8
theology, of trauma
    about, 71–75
    and anomie, 108–15
    and body-self connection,
        75–87
    and the future, 100–107
    and realism in cancer stories,
        88–89
    and resolvability, 115–17
theophany, 96
therapies, 7, 62, 68. *See also*
    treatments
Theresa of Avila, Saint, 137
Thessalonica, 148
Thompson, John, 36
Thompson, Michael, 96
touch, as healing, 138–39
transfiguration, of Jesus, 102
trauma. *See also* theology, of trauma;
    trauma, illness-related
    about, 5–7, 41–42

aftermath of, living in, 47
and crucifixion parallels, 104–5
and death, 50
language of, 54, 88, 124–25, 133
and moral evil (*see* moral evil)
and post-traumatic stress disorder
    (PTSD), 44–45
research, 64
treatment for, 47
and violence, 105
trauma, illness-related
about, 43–46
in cancer stories, 53–59
within families/friends, 66–69
and the future, 59–64
as internal threat, 47–52
religion, part in, 69–70
suffering with, 64–66
See also theology, of trauma;
    trauma
Trauma and Grace (Jones), 72
trauma and ministry
cancer stories, 11–42
church for the suffering,
    119–46
hope, 148–61
trauma, illness-related,
    43–70
trauma and theology, 71–117
treatments
chemotherapy, 21–22, 57
and grief, 34–35
immunotherapy, 28, 57
physical toll of, 18, 20–22, 38,
    51–52
psychosocial therapy, 7
and sensory perceptions, 48
stem-cell transplants, 34–35
trust, 81, 86, 148–50, 157–58

undone by cancer, 111–60

van der Kolk, Bessel, 47, 49, 62, 64,
    87, 124
victim language, 56, 111
violence, 41, 105
virtual body of Christ
visits, from the well, 129–32
vocabulary. *See* language
von Speyr, Adrienne, 110
vulnerability, 123

warrior imagery, 4, 30, 56–57, 153,
    156
When Breath Becomes Air (Kalanithi),
    11
why, asking
in Job, 92–97
and life, meaning of, 82
need for, 4
and nomos, 26–27
in the psalms, 87
and sin, 78–79
stories for, 14–15
and suffering, 65
and theodicy, 89
See also reason, cancer happens
    for a
Wiman, Christian, 37–41, 65–67, 79,
    105–6
Wolterstorff, Nicholas, 65, 154–55
women, and violence, 105
Women's Health and Cancer Rights
    Act of 1998, 50
worship
attending when ill, 122–24, 127
for families of ill, 128–29
lamentation in, 124–29
liturgy in, 124–26
technology for, 136
writing, 136

Zuidgeest, Piet, 85

CPSIA information can be obtained
at www.ICGtesting.com
Printed in the USA
BVHW040719131118
532911BV00015B/315/P

9 780664 262761